FOUNDATIONS OF THE DIGITAL STATE

Gordon Guthrie

This volume is part of series containing:

Foundations of the Digital State
ISBN: 978-1-0685451-0-8 (paperback)
ISBN: 978-1-0685451-1-5 (epub)
ISBN: 978-1-0685451-2-2 (PDF)

Working Papers Volume I - ***Foundations of the Digital State***
ISBN: 978-1-0685451-3-9 (paperback)
ISBN: 978-1-0685451-4-6 (epub)
ISBN: 978-1-0685451-5-3 (PDF)

Working Papers Volume II - ***Foundations of the Digital State***
ISBN: 978-1-0685451-6-0 (paperback)
ISBN: 978-1-0685451-7-7 (epub)
ISBN: 978-1-0685451-8-4 (PDF)

Dedicated to Orla and Sorley for putting up with me for the last 19 years thinking about this.

Foreword

A law is passed and a computer system is born.

I had the honour and privilege to be a candidate for the Scottish Parliament in 1999.

Colleagues wrote the procedures of the parliament and designed the institutions of the Scottish Government and I was able to ask them *did you design it as a mother of software?* The answer is of course, *no we didn't*. This report tries to answer the question *what would democratic institutions designed for the digital world look like?*

I drifted away from front-line electoral politics and back into a career in internet tech, but I never lost my fascination with government nor stopped thinking about the relationship between digital technology and the state, the law, the parliament.

Software has continued to eat the world, restructuring and transforming the economy. And it continues to reshape and change government.

The challenge of using technology to deliver for citizens remains, to integrate it deeply into the state. That journey starts with humility - the driving purpose is better government, not technology for its own sake.

The goal is citizens living longer, better lives, with less injustice and more opportunity for art, music, life, good jobs, security, family, friends, children, love and all that makes us human.

My 14 months at Scottish Government as a Research Fellow has been a second honour. I am grateful for the chance to study that which I know best and contribute to the future of our parliament and country for which I have a deep love and ambition.

This report provides a clear roadmap to make Scotland the finest digital state in the world and I commend it to you.

Gordon Guthrie

Research Fellow under the First Minister's Digital Fellowship Programme.

Declarations

I am grateful to the Scottish Government for the opportunity to undertake this Research Fellowship under the First Minister's Digital Fellowship scheme.

But I must point out this work is independent of Scottish Government and does not speak for them.

This report would not be possible without the myriad of people who gave me the benefit of their time and experience. The recommendations largely come from them, but the errors are mine and mine alone.

I have not received any payment (from Scottish Government or otherwise) in the course of this research.

Acknowledgements

This report could not have been written without the help and support of a large number of people. A full list of interviewees can be found in the Notes section at the end, but I would like to thank Katy McNeil and James Cattell in particular for encouraging me and including me in OneTeamGov and other activities for civil servants over many years when I was working in the private sector.

My work would not have been possible without the support of Geoff Huggins, the Chief Digital Officer at Scottish Government.

Tam McTurk and Jane Denholm fed me lunch in their flat overby from Victoria Quay and helped keep me sane.

Dawn Donaldson and I conducted a long running experiment that conclusively proved the real foundation of the digital state is a roll and sausage with a wee dod of brown, and I thank her for putting up with my chat over the past 18 months.

Notes

There are a range of notes at the end of this report covering abbreviations and terminology, naming and scope, considerations of AI and Working Papers.

The report is substantially about the rearrangement of existing work by process engineering - and is not a capital funded reform programme. It is expected to be approximately cost neutral. More discussion can be found in the note on costs.

The bulk of the technical detail and consideration of evidence is not in this report but has been written up in Working Papers, and the reader will frequently be referred to them if they wish more detail.

Contents

PART ONE

INTRODUCTION

CHAPTER ONE
Introduction

Introduction

This report focuses on developing state capability to deliver world class services underpinned by digital systems. It makes no claim for a particular outcome. Technology doesn't matter in itself, what matters is a better world for our citizens across the economy, democracy, criminal and social justice and the rest.

The journey from analogue to digital is systemic. Everything in the particular is changed and transformed by ubiquitous computing, including government, parliament and the constitution.

But the institutions and principles of the state remain. The digital state must be rooted in the rule of law, separation of powers, parliamentary oversight and democracy. The state needs to be adjusted, but not rebuilt.

The complexity of the proposed transformation in this report comes from the many small changes across different wings of the state.

This process has started, will continue, and won't stop. Scotland needs to be pro-active and not reactive.

This is not a Scottish problem and won't have a Scottish solution. This research draws on experience from all parts[1] of the globe and can be read profitably everywhere.

I have tried to keep this work below party politics. There are policy scissors - the upper blade is *policy intent* - what the government intends to happen. The lower blade is *policy effect* - what actually happens. In an ideal world these

---

[1] However it is more Anglophone than I would have liked.

scissors close - in the real world they don't.

Here better is narrowly defined as closing the gap between the blades. *Intent* is for the elected politicians, *effect* for civil servants. The goal is to increase state capability to give policy effect to policy intent more faithfully.

Politics will out though, self-denying ordinances will only take you so far.

More capability will enable new ways of thinking about policy delivery. To talk of faster state reorganisation, systemic design of state services to better include elderly, disabled or chaotic citizens, changes to the relationship between Holyrood and local government, of a faster, better cheaper way to build a new tax system, is to walk up to the door of party politics.

I invite elected politicians to enter at their own convenience.

STRUCTURE OF THE REPORT

The main body of the report falls into two parts - a description of the research process and a proposed systems design of the foundations of the digital state.

The research process covers the methodology, the evidence uncovered and issues and constraints on the final design.

Elements of the evidence are profoundly technical, across a range of disciplines. In order to make the report accessible to the general reader where ever possible the technical evidence has been pulled out into a series of working papers.

This report is ambitious and it is important to demonstrate not only the evidence but the process so that readers can make mature judgements about its recommendations.

CHAPTER TWO

Executive Summary

Executive Summary

We've had a decade of good work done and teams built. But the institutionalisation of it, I think, is the hard work for the next little bit.

Hilary Hartley
former Deputy Digital Minister, Ontario

The problems that this report is trying to address can be summarised as:

The government needs a single organisation with the mechanism to make decisions about **how** *digital systems should work, and parliament needs a single structure to oversee those decisions.*

Decisions about **what** *digital systems should do are made sub-optimally by parliament using ad-hoc repurposed mechanisms.*

The state lacks a research capability for digital systems.

This report lays out a roadmap to make Scotland the best digital state in the world. It addresses these 3 problems and is backed by evidence and based on extensive research and experience.

Recommendations

It makes 26 recommendations and proposes 10 legislative enactments over 3 to 5 years. Those enactments will be consolidated into a much smaller number of bills.

The recommendations span the entire political system, from measures that would help think-tanks and political parties get a better understanding of how the digital state works, changes to parliamentary procedures and the structure of Bill Packs and legislation alike, through new government and parliamentary institutions to the organisation and responsibilities of the civil service.

The recommendations fall under 3 major headings:

1. unitary specification of services and systems - the **how**
2. better iteration in service development - the **what**
3. developing a research capability - the **research**

Unitary specification involves creating new institutions - one of them becoming the technical leadership of the civil service.

It is appropriate that that body supervises both *Better Iteration* and *Developing A Research Capability*.

These recommendations combine to make a coherent system design, and incorporate a theory of state for the digital age. The implementation and roll-out is complex and will be iterative.

The recommendations span the executive, legislature and, indirectly, the judiciary. Implementation needs to have a constitutional and not a party flavour.

SCALE OF THE IMPACT

This report is explicitly ambitious. It recommends institutional changes which are intended to endure for at least 100 years.

These changes for parliament and government are on a par with the creation of the Scottish Law Commission. The work is substantive but not overwhelming. It is an adjustment but not a reconstruction.

Conceptual basis

There are two separate types of specification for computers systems:

- ***functional*** specifications which describe ***what*** the system does
- ***non-functional*** or ***infrastructural*** specifications which describe ***how*** it does it

Close examination of the 3 social security acts and the 76 pieces of secondary legislation about Scottish Social security conclusively demonstrate that specification is partial.

Primary legislation contains the functional specification - but the non-functional or infrastructural specification is scattered over Scottish and UK government guidelines and standards, partly codified best-practice and departmental ways of working.

In the old world, say the 1950s, the infrastructure for social security (buildings with canteens, roofs and windows, on a bus route) was totally decoupled from the functionality of the administrative process (forms and calculations).

In the new world there are additional non-functional and infrastructure considerations: sign-ons, databases and backup, cybersecurity, joined-up government and data sharing. This is tightly coupled with the functional administrative software but lacks any institutional deliberative and enforcement apparatus comparable to legislation and judicial review.

UNITARY SPECIFICATION OF SERVICES AND SYSTEMS

This stream of work addresses the non-functional or infrastructural problem. It is about changing how the state makes decisions about ***how*** digital systems should work.

This part of the report recommends two new institutions.

The first is a government body - the Digital Services Reform Office (DSRO). In its work and remit it rhymes with the Scottish Law Commission. The DRSO has the power to issue technical standards and recommend both legislative changes and programmes of work. These activities need to be adopted by the government of the day to proceed.

The second is a parliamentary body - the Digital Services Scrutiny & Audit Commission (DSS&AC). It works under the supervision of a parliamentary committee. In its scrutiny work it rhymes with the Scottish Commission on Social Security and it its audit work it rhymes with Audit Scotland.

The two streams, functional and non-functional & infrastructural specification come together in the Bill Pack. Legislation continues to specify the functionality that state computer systems must implement. An additional Systems Impact Assessment in the Bill Pack addresses the non-functional or institutional requirements. It lists what data must be reused, what technical standards the new systems must adhere to, which supporting functions (payments, sign-on and identity, etc) are to be used.

However, the two parts of the specification have different development cycles. The functional specifications are system specific and go through the normal legislative process. The non-functional or infrastructure specifications are shared across the public sector and require an entirely different development and oversight process.

Critically the process of creating the technical standards that underpin the non-functional or infrastructural requirements will be led by technical specialists - with oversight provided by other experts who report to the parliament and not the government.

The standards-based approach is modelled on the standards regime of the internet, which enables co-ordination without communication and have proved spectacularly successful.

This institutional approach makes possible the unity of specification when the minister introduces the bill.

A full list of the recommendations and legislative enactments supporting this work please is appended to the Executive Summary.

Better iteration in service development

This stream of work addresses the issue of how the state can better make decisions about ***what*** state digital systems do.

Iteration is the super-power of the internet age, testing plans against reality. Building physical infrastructure is a monolithic and ***complicated*** process - but one that is amenable to up-front planning. A project can be specified, broken down into tasks and sub-tasks which can be scheduled and costed.

This approach was initially attempted with software, and has been everywhere abandoned, even in government. Small-a agile[2] is now a mantra.

Software development is fundamentally ***complex***. It changes the team making it and the organisation implementing it. It changes the behaviour of citizens, and it changes the basic understanding of the problem. Testing assumptions early and then changing course is the proven way forward.

The quicker you test things with real people, the quicker you find errors and shortcomings and the quicker you fix them. It's simply cheaper, much cheaper.

But agile in government starts too late. This report recommends a set of immediate changes and a more strategic long term ones.

The first pass of improving iteration is to bring design and testing activities from the end of the process to the beginning. For major projects prototype systems should be developed before legislation is drafted. These would have limited functionality, not be scalable, or perhaps just be paper prototypes. Policy and delivery teams need to be integrated.

On first glance, the legislative process puts iteration into the deep freeze. Once the law is the law, the systems must comply with it. Close examination shows that major systems like Universal Credit or Scottish Social Security have a more continuous specification of functionality - and the mechanism used is just secondary legislation. The recommendations include making legislative iteration a first class and, crucially, designed process.

Shifting these activities affects not just how the state is

---

[2] Big-A Agile is a particular software development methodology with its own rules and rituals

organised, but parliamentary oversight, public engagement. It presents a host of delicate political and constitutional issues. As such it must be approached carefully and in an appropriate cross-party manner.

The bulk of the work falls on the government side, and this work will be overseen by the institution created for better specification - the DSRO.

A full list of the recommendations and legislative enactments supporting this work please is appended to the Executive Summary.

Developing a Research Capability

Unitary Specification and *Better Iteration* both involve building capability of the state. That will enable a more ambitious digital future. Scotland needs to start planning to use it to be more ambitious.

There are two elements to the research brief. The first is small teams of 3 or 4, with 6 to 9 month briefs to research and prototype new ways of organising the state. It will be delivered by CivTech, the Scottish Government's innovation arm - moving its work earlier in governmental processes. The proposed topics are:

- *Rules as Code*
- *Generating MVPs as part of policy and legislative design*
- *Macro-economic modelling*
- *Property-based testing*
- *Components*
- *Remixability*
- *Revisiting on-prem and global scale capacity*

But there are additional strategic research programmes covering:

- a law reform process for data
- a review of legislative processes for major digital programmes
- a review of legislative process for local government and other sub-state bodies

A full list of the recommendations and legislative enactments supporting this work please is appended to the Executive Summary.

Implementation

The implementation plan uses existing powers of the Scottish Parliament and Government to create shadow versions of the final state organisations on both the parliamentary and civil service side.

The Scottish parliament will use existing powers to co-opt external experts as advisers. The Scottish Government will second civil servants, bolstered by external expertise recruited under the existing First Ministers Digital Fellowship Programme.[3]

The parliamentary side of the work will be overseen by a special committee which will represent the Scottish Parliament Corporate Body in the discussions with Ministers.

That committee will create temporary procedures of the Scottish Parliament to pilot the new ways of working, new forms of the Bill Pack and so on, and take individual bills through parliament in the new way. This process will be

3 This research was conducted under the First Minster's Digital Fellowship Programme.

iterative.

Once there is consensus and agreement across the political divide the task of drawing up the legislative enactments and changes to parliamentary standing orders, and taking them through parliament will be on the committee. The government will play an appropriate supporting role.

Where the work touches on the format of legislation, in particular the law reform proposal, it would be appropriate for the Scottish Law Commission to bring it's expertise to bear.

Costs

The recommendations fall into one of the following five categories:

- do what we currently do, but in a different sequence
- do what we currently do, but in a different part of the organisation
- do what we currently do, but under different rules
- do what we currently do, but more consistently
- do what we currently do, but with greater velocity

This report will be approximately cost neutral. The Scottish Government spends, acknowledged or not, about 15% of its IT budget on routine maintenance and addressing technical debt. This long-running and continued spend is the basis for bringing existing systems into compliance with the new proposed standards regime.

None of the recommendations involve capital programmes.

Skills

During my interviews I found no evidence that there are significant skills gaps between civil servants and the major internet companies I have worked in. There is no magic just-one-trick or flash-of-light methodology that will unlock the digital state.

The impact of implementing this report

This report focuses on foundational changes that support the infrastructural underpinnings of the digital state.

The changes will provide the capacity and competencies needed to make Scotland the best digital state in the world and their impact will be felt in a variety of ways.

Empower the wider political class

Leadership from the top will be essential on this journey. Nobody goes into politics to make a worse Scotland, all politicians are ambitious for the better, although they disagree on how and why.

Changing the context in which political decisions are taken is a major focus of this report.

25 years into the parliament it is time to take stock and re-assess:

- the information we publish that helps the wider political class understand where Scotland stands on digital.
- the institutions that propose and develop technical options to the point that they are amenable to scrutiny and supervision by the parliament and government.
- the support we provide to parliamentarians, whether in opposition or government, in their decision-making and scrutiny for services based on digital systems
- the provision of the right information, at the right time, in the right format to decision makers.
- the design of the processes and structures that parliamentarians live within to be the most effective ways of creating new services based on digital systems.
- the mechanisms by which civic society can understand and critique our digital services and cultivate proposals to make them better and generate political pressure to implement them.

The reasons for this disempowerment are structural and the root of this problem is three-fold.

Firstly, timing. Holyrood and the modern digital world were born about the same time. In 1999 the digital future was but dimly emerging and the implications of the modern internet for society and the economy were far from clear.

Secondly we (the political class) have not reviewed our constitutional and institutional assumptions in light of the development of the digital world.

Thirdly we (the technical class) have not articulated our

requirements about the structure and flow of decision-making in political and constitutional terms. The technical class within the civil service are bound by constitutional taboos, it is not their place to boss ministers and parliamentarians around. We (the technical class out in the private sector) have largely kept our distance, failed to engage with and understand how and why government works, and contributed platitudes.

This report does not shy from recommending changes to the structure and working of parliament, the organisation of legislation, the machinery of government, accountability lines and the relationships of civil servants to ministers and parliament alike, or changes to the technical and policy trades.

Fix structural problems

Infrastructure and functionality were uncoupled in the old analogue state. In the digital age infrastructure and functionality are mixed together in software.

Simply by building an institution to conceive, plan, design and maintain that infrastructure, and another to provide political oversight and audit, Scotland can take a lead.

There are simple steps to better, more usable state websites and joined up systems that ask for information once and work together.

Fixing the structural problem will enable the empowerment of our political class by changing what the politicians discuss and when they discuss it - moving oversight from abstract principles to concrete systems.

Change when decisions are being made

The structure of legislative decision-making is changing from a 13th century model to a 21st century one - Social Security Scotland shows the way. That programme has had 3 primary Acts of parliament and 76 pieces of secondary legislation over 6 years.

That planned legislative programme learned as much from Universal Credit as possible. The challenge is to generalise that learning, to switch from the particulars of Social Security to the general of legislative decision-making for major software systems.

It should start with a smaller bill that authorises and funds basic design, prototyping and testing, before moving onto the main bill later. This will change the context of parliamentary oversight. Parliamentarians and stakeholders will spend more time discussing a shared tangible thing. At the moment each MSP has to conjure a system from their reading of legislation and argue over who has the better imagining of it.

At its heart, this approach simply redistributes parliamentary oversight from points in time where it can't be effective in shaping the systems to ones where it can.

Do less, get more (reduce costs and get better government)

Digital technology is opaque and hard to reason about. You can't see it, taste it, touch it or smell it. You can only use it. And you can only use it when it is in a working state. For big bang implementations that is when it is finished.

Iterative working, building the smallest working thing and

asking "is this what we really wanted" is about making the opaque visible. Moving to more iterative approaches has already saved the UK and Scottish governments millions and delivered immense benefits. The shorter the iterative cycle, the less the programme can go off course, the shorter the course correction, the less rework, the less cost. And the less rework and correction the teams are doing, the more time they have to concentrate on citizens needs. Focusing on iterative speed and responsiveness creates a virtuous circle of better systems, built more cheaply and more quickly.

Thinking systematically about it, and making strategic changes to the format of bills and bill packs and planning major software developments as iterative sequences of legislative acts will unlock these benefits.

Better iteration and better and more appropriate feedback loops to connect politicians, policy makers and citizens will improve the political class's understanding of the impact of policy, and ultimately improve the quality of policy making itself.

The recommendations improve iteration without compromising parliamentary scrutiny.

Do less, get more (reuse data and get more joined up government)

Iteration can reduce *rework,* but it can't reduce *work*. Only data consolidation can do that. The same data in 2 places needs 2 sets of administrators and has twice the data maintenance costs. Duplicated data generates its own work on top of that - in reconciliation, correction and data matching.

The institutions this report recommends will be able to understand the data landscape and co-ordinate the organisational, legislative and technical changes required to reorganise the state to eliminate data duplication. That simplification will improve data quality and benefit everyone.

Improve outcomes

The 3rd major benefit of eliminating rework is better outcomes. Shorter iterative cycles means more contact with citizens and end-users and less time focusing on internal issues of the state.

The goal here is not to deliver *a single better outcome*, but to improve all outcomes across the piece by systematically changing how the civil service works. Rework and correction is always a waste of resources that should be put to better use.

Empower citizens, society and businesses

The state is the servant of the citizens. The state collects and organises, but also hordes, much data.

That data needs to be opened up for citizens and companies to use - not statically as spreadsheets, but as Application Programmable Interfaces (APIs) for building things: travel apps, planning portals or land usage sites.

The recommended institutions and changes are a systematic and institutional approach to maximising the utility of state data for society.

DO THINGS WE CURRENTLY CAN'T DO

The more capability the state has, the more opportunities are unlocked. Scotland should prepare to exploit this.

If we can generate proof-of-concept software directly from legislation we can improve decision-making. Draft legislation can be explored by examining systems that implement it.

Regulation is popular (stop sofas burning) but regulatory compliance costs aren't (red tape). The internet shows another way. A simple web page must comply with about 1.7 million words of technical standards. But a teenager can build a compliant website just by using software (browsers, web servers, javascript frameworks, test runners, etc) that embed the standards.

This is a big tech company superpower - turning process compliance into software. *This must be checked, that must be checked, this must happen, that must not happen* - all implemented in code, press button compliance.

Scotland should be researching how to develop ease-of-compliance legislation.

The state is where the citizens are - and the citizens are on screens now, mostly, But there will always be people who struggle with screens, because they are old, they are disabled or their lives are chaotic. We need to systematically research how to blend on-screen and in-person support for state services - and solve that problem once for Scotland and not once for every service.

With new institutions and standards we can make the state more malleable by building systems from components and platforms, that can be stood up, stood down, changed and recombined and remixed as circumstances change.

The tools to build the future

Digital systems are not a fad, they are the fabric of modern life and the sooner we start laying the foundations of the digital state the better we can start benefiting from the use of technology.

The recommendations of this report provide a blueprint for those foundations. Scottish politics should rise to the occasion and help make Scotland the best digital state in the world.

This work is not going to go away, it will endure, now is the time to start.

Recommendations

The recommendations are organised by which part of the full political-legislative-in-service cycle they impact. Each recommendation is marked as **what, how** or **research** appropriately.

In-service recommendations

1 an obligation to publish non-functional & infrastructural statistics about state operations - **what**

2 Registers of Services, Powers and Policies - **what**

Election and politics recommendations

3 widening access to data - **what**

4 - widening access to research fellowships - **what**

5 - Short money considerations - **what**

Government institutions and the programme for government recommendations

6 - create a Digital Services Reform Office - how

6.1 - the foundations of the DSRO - how

6.2 - changes to the PLU's Bill Handbook - what

6.3 - improved organisational support for the PLU and Bill Teams - what

6.4 - make non-functional & infrastructural work visible in the Programme for Government - what

6.5 - a law reform process for data - research

6.6 - the development and proposition of Machinery of Government changes - what

6.7 - run the strategic research programme and commission new research - research

6.8 - participation in a joint review of legislative processes with the parliament - research

6.9 - a user-centred design roadshow - what

6.10 - an information architecture - what

7 - review the process of creating legislation for local government and other sub-state bodies - **research**

The Bill Pack, etc recommendations

8 - changes to the Bill Pack, etc - how

8.1 - changes to the Bill Pack for primary legislation - how

8.2 - changes to the Explanatory Notes for secondary legislation - how

8.3 - approvals process for day-to-day services implementation - **how**

9 a new gazette to publish technical standards in - **how**

Parliamentary institutions and processes

10 create a Digital Services Audit & Scrutiny Commission - how

11 a review of legislative processes for major digital programmes - research

12 publication of legislative amendments - what

13 additional capabilities for SPICe - **what**

Testing recommendations

14 testing needs to be made a first class professional discipline in Government - **what**

Delivery recommendations

15 changes to lines of responsibility in the civil service - **how**

Legislative enactments required

The following legislative enactments will be required. These separate enactments will be bundled into a smaller number of Bills and will be introduced in Committee and not as Government Bills.

1 putting the Digital Services Reform Office on a statutory basis

2 putting the Digital Services Scrutiny & Audit Commission on a statutory basis

3 an Enabling Act

4 new register of services

5 new register of powers

6 new register of policy
7 amendments to The Interpretation And Legislative Reform (Scotland) Act 2010
8 obligation to publish data
9 obligation to publish non-functional statistics
10 a Data Bill of Rights

In addition Recommendation 11 may also require technical changes to Section 36[4] of the Scotland Act 1998.

Conclusion

This report recommends 3 interlocking system redesigns. These improve both ***what*** the state does through services built on top of digital systems and ***how*** it does it. In addition it recommends building a small and focused strategic research function to maximise the impact of these new capabilities.

These recommendations are evidenced, prudential and precedented. They are cost neutral, strategic and institutional. They have been designed with a 100 year impact in view - but will start delivering immediate benefit.

4 https://www.legislation.gov.uk/ukpga/1998/46/section/36

Part Two

Process

CHAPTER THREE

Introduction to the process

Introduction

This part of the report documents the research process that drove the design of the new systems.

It outlines the methodology used, including the analytical approach, interview design and participant selection.

It then walks through the evidence iteratively. The technical details and discussion of theory of state are documented separately in a series of Working Papers. The reader is invited to follow the references to them in the text.

Finally it documents the constraints under which the system design must operate and the precedents that were consulted in the design process.

CHAPTER FOUR
Methodology

The starting point

The research started with a research proposal and some axioms and hypotheses. Both are reproduced in the Appendix 1 - *Digital Fellowship Research Proposal* and Appendix 2 - *Digital Fellowship research axioms and hypotheses*.

The proposal was holistic: going from manifesto and think tank, through policy development, the *Programme For Government*[5] (and the legislative programme it contains), bills and bill packs, parliamentary procedures, through the design-test-deliver cycle and onto in-service where the snake eats its own tail. Politics begins with the state-as-it-is.

It was practitioner-led with structured interviews with participants from around that cycle and relevant academics.

The interviewees were from both Scotland and furth of Scotland. The results are globally applicable, Scotland is merely the site of the research.

Two research axioms were proposed:

- the Scottish political class are not good enough customers of digital services (yet). Prior to 1983 almost no legislation anywhere in the world led to the creation of a computer system, now almost no legislation doesn't. Systems do not optimally do things they were not designed to
- we already have the answers, we don't necessarily know it

---

5 This is a Scottish Government process - see the Note on terms

The starting point was to test the veracity of the four hypotheses:

- continuous improvement via process re-ordering will identify defects earlier, reduce iteration time and lead to better outcomes
- the legislative process contains hidden barriers to modernisation
- legislation implicitly defines data and hence processes in the administrative state
- the audit structure for administrative legislation needs to be extended

These hypotheses were evidenced, principally from detailed study of the Gershon[6] and Bichard[7] reports that I did when I first attempted this project back in 2005.

A number of precepts were brought to the process:

1. *against detachment*
2. *people rarely fail, processes often fail*
3. *experience over seniority.*
4. *pro synthesis, contra innovation*
5. *a prejudice for precedents*
6. *an unnatural love for the Goldilocks question*
7. *pro core competencies*
8. *contra reading over from the private sector*
9. *contra centralisation and central planning*
10. *build a simple working system first*

The last of these particularly applies to the implementation plan of this report. The recommendations

6 https://www.civilservant.org.uk/library/2004_gershon_releasing_resources_to_the_front_line.pdf

7 https://dera.ioe.ac.uk/id/eprint/6394/1/report.pdf

will be rolled out and tested iteratively. The working system is the system we have now, the journey to the future is continuous, incremental improvement. It is drawn out of the common clay as the pot from the lump on the potter's wheel.

These precepts are discussed more fully in Appendix 3 - *Research precepts*.

The Northecote-Trevelyan[8] report of 1854 is the model for this review. It is often presented as a discontinuous event with a before of corruption, nepotism and civil service ineptitude, contrasting with an after of excellence and probity.

The reality is blended. Northecote and Trevelyan make clear that they are systematisers. They reviewed staffing, recruitment and promotional policies on a department by department basis. Their report is a synthesis of best practices from across the Home and Indian Civil Services.

This report shamelessly synthesises the expertise and insights of civil servants from all over the world.

The only innovation comes from the systems thinking. Innovation and problem solving among practitioners around the world have created localised and departmental best practices. This report makes of them a systemic programme of institutional change.

In 1911 Lloyd George laid the foundations of the Welfare State. He wrote the legislation and personally designed the paper forms. They were still called Lloyd George forms when they were transposed into data tables and forms in the first GP management systems in the 1980s. Lloyd George's designs

---

8 https://www.civilservant.org.uk/library/1854_Northcote_Trevelyan_Report.pdf

were, and remain, unintentionally foundational to the modern GP service 123 years later.

That insight is the source of the clear-eyed ambition of this report - the impact of decisions being made now about foundational data and digital infrastructure will be visible in 123 years also. Those decisions could be, should be and must be intentional.

Explicite, Constitutionnalité et Simplicité

Early on in the process, three guiding principles emerged with have shaped both the engagement and the recommendations: *Explicite, Constitutionnalité et Simplicité*.

Explicite

Systems must be documented so that participants can understand their role and participate in continuous improvement.

Everybody in the end-to-end cycle, from politics to in-service plays their part, and needs to understand their role in the whole cycle explicitly.

The glory of the outcomes cannot be separated from the grind of the delivery.

Constitutionnalité

The digital revolution has increased the power of the state[9] - and citizens need to be protected from that.

The government can, should and must only act under the rule of law. Parliament needs to have the capability to hold

9 It has granted private sector players immense and unacceptable powers too vis-à-vis the individual

them accountable.

Software development processes must be moulded to constitutional norms

SIMPLICITÉ

Gall's famous law[10] states that a complex system that works is invariably found to have evolved from a simple system that works.

The implementation plan of this report builds a small working system first and then incrementally grows that, testing each new element as it develops.

These three maxims shape this work profoundly.

---

10 See Appendix 3 - *Research precepts*

The foundational process cycle

The conceptual framework is a recursive cycle, a snake eating its own tail, an ouroboros of politics, policy, legislation and operations. The interviewees are suggested by it and the interviews structured by it.

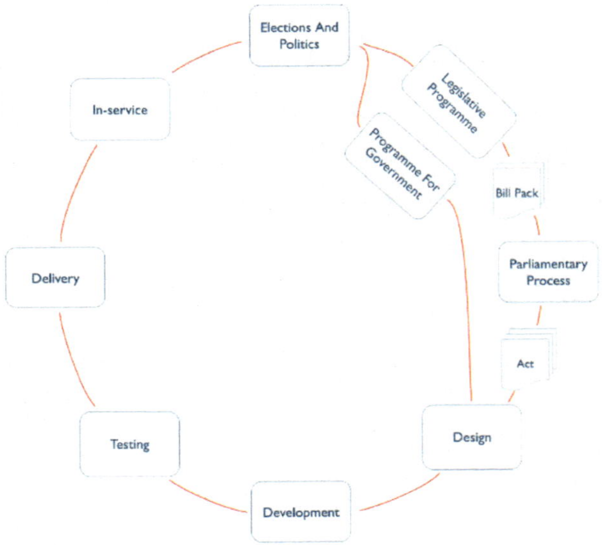

It starts at *In-Service* - the cycle begins with how things are now.

Pressure to change comes from *Politics* in the form of *Elections* with many actors: parties, thinktanks, opinion formers, trade organisations, third sector, and civic society in the widest sense.

The government prepares a *Programme for Government* (including a *Legislative Programme*). It is a rolling work plan for the coming year and into the mid-term. Only a fraction of this is relevant to this research programme.

For some work streams Bills (primary legislation) or

Ministerial Orders (secondary legislation) are prepared with their supporting materials - a *Bill Pack*.

Those legal proposals go through one of the *Parliamentary Processes* defined in the Standing Orders of the Scottish Parliament and become *Acts* (or *Orders* in the case of secondary legislation).

But a large amount of policy work is under existing powers and bypasses the parliamentary cycle.

Relevant changes then go through a normal software development cycle *Design*, *Development*, *Testing*, *Delivery* and the cycle starts again at In-Service.

This foundation process definition means that:

- a programme of interviews could be developed and checked for completeness
- a model for assessing whether *the right thing was being done at the right time* could be developed.

The foundational process diagram is also explicit. Parliament and politics are traditionally no-go areas for civil servants. Here everything is on the table.

It has separation of powers at it heart - it is constitutional.

Interviewee selection and interviews

65 people had a structured interviewed, and I had directed conversations with another 27. Several hundred have participated in less formal group discussions, seen talks or presentations. Working papers were written and published throughout the process and garnered an audience of readers and commentators.

About 70% of the interviewees are from Scotland, with

20% from Westminster/England and 10% from the rest of world - mostly Anglophone countries.

The interviews in Scotland covered the entire foundational process cycle. Outside Scotland people with interesting things to say were sought out.

Interviewees included manifesto writers, policy civil servants, Ministers, SPADs, MSPs (opposition and government backbench), designers of all types (service, UX, organisation, content), technical and business architects, data specialists in local and central/Scottish government, auditors, law commission members, parliamentary clerks, agency executives, delivery and in-service managers.

A full list of interviewees and the role for which they were selected can be found in the Notes Section.

Interviews were conducted in an approximate Japanese order (juniors to seniors) - where proximity to the charismatic class (Ministers and MSPs) is the mark of seniority.

The research was practitioner-led. Each structured interview followed the same format. The cycle was outlined and the interviewee was asked to describe their role in that cycle, their contents and discontents with their upstreams and downstreams, and from that a dialogue would flow.

The interviews threw up topics to follow up in the literature as well as open questions. Individuals who could illuminate those questions were sought out for interview. Literature was chased down and read.

Root causes were sought - by recursively questioning and challenging the definition of problems. This approach was based on the insights of Taiichi Ohno and the Toyota

Production System[11].

[11] Ohno, T. (1988). Toyota Production System : beyond large-scale Production. London: Crc Press.

CHAPTER FIVE
Evidence

Introduction

This chapter will discuss the evidence that the research turned up. Detailed discussion of technical elements is in various working papers and appendices and will be referenced as appropriate.

The evidence is presented as a linear narrative. Needless to say the process of unearthing it was far more haphazard. There were dead ends and side quests. Some paths were revisited in light of new understanding.

There are several threads chased down iteratively:

- exploring the initial hypotheses
- exploring iteration
- functional and non-functional & infrastructure specification

A number of other issues were explored in an ad-hoc manner.

First thread - exploring the initial hypotheses

Introduction

The initial interviews were set up around the hypotheses in the research proposal[12].

The starting point was anecdotal and formed from discussions at One Team Gov and UKGovCamp and other civil servant networking activities over many years. The consensus was that best practice consists of integrated policy and delivery teams, defining outcomes and measurements up front and iterating on policy development in the context of

[12] See Appendix 2 - Digital Fellowship research axioms and hypotheses

existing systems. But best practice is far from common practice - and the strongest advocates for it come from the technical and design side, not the policy side.

The overriding theme emerging from the technical and delivery practitioner interviews was *speak to us sooner*.

From data specialists, to technical experts, from statistics, content, design, there was a recurring call to be involved earlier in the policy process.

By contrast the most common response of interviewees from the politics/policy side was that *technology happens after we do our bit*.

First iteration - why is there such a disconnect between politics/policy and the technical/design/delivery teams?

To understand the policy world better I did the Bill Team training as a proxy[13] for how the policy teams think of digital. This is a yearly programme run by the Legislation and Parliament Unit (LPU) with 12 sessions. The bill process itself is described in the LPU's *Bill Handbook*[14]. Neither the seminar series nor the *Bill Handbook* discuss delivery questions, reuse of existing digital systems and data, iteration or integration of technology into policy development.

The external presenters at the bill training echoed the cry

---

13 There are 3 parallel streams of work that delivery policy via technology. At the top end is a new Bill, in the middle is Ministerial Orders that change the context of existing Acts and at the bottom is day to day work. This work used the first as a proxy to understand the other two.

14 https://www.gov.scot/binaries/content/documents/govscot/publications/foi-eir-release/2022/07/foi-202200306018/documents/foi-202200306018---information-released/foi-202200306018---information-released/govscot:document/FOI%2B202200306018%2B-%2BInformation%2Breleased.pdf

of the technical interviewees, imploring the bill teams to talk to them as early as possible.

This isn't a peculiarly Scottish problem - equivalents to the Bill Handbook are published by Westminster[15] and Cardiff[16], although tracking down the one at Stormont eluded me. They also don't discuss technology, data and infrastructural systems reuse.

Civil servant technical and design teams are heavily influenced by iteration and testing practices in the private sector.

Policy teams aren't so influenced, nor are they trained to think that way - and so they don't. Some are integrated with design and delivery, but some continue developing policy and throwing it over the wall to be implemented.

More details can be found in Section 5 - Current State in Working Paper 10.2 - *Immediate Hygienic Measures*.

Second iteration - why is there no pressure to integrate policy/delivery from the ministerial leadership?

Ministers, MSPs (government and opposition), SPADs, thinktankers and manifesto writers were interviewed. Broadly the political class agree with the policy people that things are handed over to delivery to be implemented, and that their role substantially is disconnected from that.

However digging into the deployment of Social Security a slightly different picture emerged. The Scottish Social

---

15 https://assets.publishing.service.gov.uk/media/62fe365fe90e0703e1bb4844/2022-08_Guide_to_Making_Legislation_-_master_version__4_.pdf

16 https://www.gov.wales/sites/default/files/publications/2024-06/legislation-handbook-senedd-bills.pdf

Security programme was very mindful of the history of Universal Credit, and its two false starts. Great effort was made to learn from those lessons and think about delivery early. This caution fed through into later stages of Social Security when new functionality was being added - functionality specified in Ministerial Orders. Care was taken to engage with the delivery side in this. Even then there remained a disconnect with commencement dates for new functional Ministerial Orders not aligning with the delivery dates for the software. If a function goes live now in law and the software to support it goes live later, then an inefficient, expensive and potentially error-prone manual work-around is required to bridge the gap.

The political class can be persuaded of the necessity of best practice in a particular case if there is a sufficiently large comparative disaster, but have not internalised that and demanded it everywhere.

THIRD ITERATION - WHY IS THERE NO EXTERNAL POLITICAL PRESSURE FOR A DIFFERENT APPROACH TO DIGITAL?

Manifesto writers and think-tankers were interviewed, in Scotland and at Westminster. There was a consensus across the manifesto writers that manifestos have two parts - a defence against questions section, and a retail offering to voters.

The defence against questions are all about costings, tax and spend. This is the major vulnerability of political parties in election campaigns. There is a rich body of organisations that have opinions on tax and spend, which study the published data and analyse money. This ecosystem enables journalists to ask difficult questions - and the manifesto writer is obliged to fashion armour against these attacks.

By contrast the retail offering to voters section is much more sales and marketing. Digital, which ought to feature on the tax and spend side as the primary mechanism for better outcomes and lower costs, appears only on the retail offering side. *Great things will happen when public services have the latest hot tech rubbed on them* where the hot tech is variously e-government, shared services, blockchain or currently AI. There will be questions about how much it will cost, but few questions about how likely it is to succeed.

Fourth iteration - why is there no analytical ecosystem that supports journalists asking questions?

Leaving aside the very real challenge of the collapse of a functioning Scottish Press ecosystem, there is a real problem with digital audit. The financial audit mechanisms have slowly grown over the last century or so into the modern system. Detailed financial reports are published on a statutory basis, backed by long running statistical series. There are academic and research disciplines around them.

There is no equivalent for digital services. There is no single register of services - what does the Scottish government expose to whom digitally? The Scottish Government doesn't know, let alone the press and the opposition.

Conclusions

There are a series of interlocking failures in process. Substantially there is no directed political pressure for improvement of digital services. Criticism of government digital provision take the form of I-was-on-holiday-in-X-whyoh-why? anecdotes which are unfocused. Journalists are unaware of what questions to ask, and have no underlying audit information to work from. The political class is unaware of how to organise innovative policy work that will be implemented in parts in digital services.

There is no shortage of expertise in the civil service to help address or raise these issues, but civil servants are hamstrung by central taboos of the modern civil service.

It is not a civil servant's place to step over the line between politics and public service, nor is their place to develop a critique of parliamentary process.

Second thread - exploring iteration

Introduction

One of the axioms of this research process is that *systems don't optimally do that which they were not designed to do*, and that *the processes at Holyrood were not designed to specify digital systems.*

Iteration clearly happens and it was important to understand how that occurs.

The major iterative software project in Scotland post-devolution is Social Security Scotland - born in the Social Security (Scotland) Act 2012.[17]

It in turn drew heavily on the lessons of Universal Credit - a major UK digital programme arising out of the Welfare Reform Act 2012[18].

UC ran into trouble. Many parties contributed to the turn

---

17 https://www.legislation.gov.uk/asp/2018/9/contents

18 https://www.legislation.gov.uk/ukpga/2012/5/contents

around, internally from the Department of Work and Pensions (DWP), Her Majesty's Revenue and Customs (HMRC) as key partners, the Local Government Association (LGA) and the Government Digital Service (GDS). They reorganised the development methodologies of the programme. Critically the technique of incremental development and always-be-working systems in front of users became the gold standard.

GDS went on to become one of the most globally influential organisations in digital government and a font of experience and insight.

Members of the original GDS team moved into the private sector and provided consultancy, including for the creation of Ontario Digital Services.

Lets revisit those stories chronologically.

First iteration - Universal Credit

Universal Credit had a number of false starts before GDS were called in to rescue it. It has been designed as a big bang problem and an unrealistic Go Live! date had emerged by some unknown mechanism.

Iteration in Universal Credit was substantially accomplished by means of secondary legislation. In the 12 years after the passing of the basic foundational Act, 218 different pieces of secondary legislation were passed - about one and a half orders a week. Commencement orders, pilot programmes and ramped transitions from old benefits to new were used to break functionality up, deliver it incrementally in working, but partial, systems and test.

This iteration is overseen by a Social Security Commission which has a special role of assessing secondary legislation before it is laid.

Second iteration - Scottish Social Security

The story of Scotland is less interesting. As with UC, there were 78 pieces of secondary legislation in 6 years - about 1 a month. Whereas UC was creating a new system, and therefore its functionality had to be developed, Scottish Social Security had a mission to clone existing UK benefits. The cloned products were to have the ability to change and evolve post-launch. But the substantial task of discovery, which iteration is required for, was absent.

The normal Scottish Parliament procedures were followed for Scottish Social Security - with the exception of the creation of a new Social Security Commission (based on the existing Westminster one). This has an oversight role for Scottish social security ministerial orders.

A detailed section by section reading of all 79 pieces of Scottish Social Security legislation triggered a major quantitative study of how legislation specifies services and the digital systems they are built on - which is the subject of the third thread.

Third iteration - Ontario Digital Services

Ontario also built on the lessons of GDS/UC. In their case a readiness assessment process was put in place - which included pre-legislative checks. Projects were assessed as to whether their teams had the right composition (integrated policy/delivery), had used appropriate citizen consultation/policy development techniques, had defined desired outcomes and measures to assess success or failure and so on.

Fourth iteration - evaluating parliamentary processes

There is a substantial literature about the failings of secondary legislation, with the Hansard Society in the vanguard. The history of the development of the modern bill pack and financial statements was explored.

Conclusion

Major software projects are delivered iteratively in a naive fashion via secondary legislation. There has been no substantial re-evaluation of legislative and oversight processes for the digital era.

Iteration was imposed on UC by the technologists, occasioned by a series of delivery crises. It has political salience, and will continue to do so as long as the memory remains fresh. The lessons have not been institutionalised.

These issues are discussed at length in Working Paper 7.3 *Experimental digital legislative processes* - which looks at GDS/UC, Scottish Social Security, Ontario Digital Services and the Hansard Society critique of secondary legislation in greater detail. Working Paper 10.2 *Immediate hygienic measures* covers the history of the Bill Pack.

Third thread - functional and non-functional and infrastructure requirements

Introduction

It is in this thread that the fundamental split in this report occurs - the split between ***what*** state digital systems do and ***how*** they do it. That split is evidenced by quantitative evidence contained in Working Paper 9.1 *Reading legislation with a non-functional eye.*

The critical analytical difference had been spotted earlier in Working Paper 2 *Rules as code* but it took a while for the penny to drop. That process is documented in Working Paper X *The heart of the beast* which perhaps gives an indication of the importance of this subject.

To recapitulate there is a tension between 2 aspects of specification of computer systems - the ***what*** and the ***how***.

What the systems does is the functional specification and ***how*** it does it is the non-functional or infrastructure specification.

It is best to work from an example. Consider Section 77 of the Social Security (Scotland) Act 2018[19] which imposes a duty to consider effects of inflation.

It starts with:

> *(1) Before the end of each financial year, the Scottish Ministers must—*
>
> > *(a) calculate the inflation-adjusted level of each relevant figure,*

---

19 https://www.legislation.gov.uk/asp/2018/9/introduction/enacted

This is a specification. A software developer has to write the code to deal with this, indeed the legislation contains a formula in sub-section 4. It's a functional specification - it states ***what*** the software must do.

Compare this to Section 7:

> *In fulfilling their duty under section 3(a), the Scottish Ministers must have regard to the possibility that information obtained for the purpose of determining an individual's eligibility for one type of assistance might be used to identify the individual's eligibility for other types of assistance.*

This too is a specification, code must be written. But it is a non-functional or infrastructure specification - it describes ***how*** the software must work.

The Act also contains lots of sections that aren't specification at all, for instance Section 1 which starts:

> *The Scottish social security principles are—*
>
> > *(a) social security is an investment in the people of Scotland,*
> >
> > *(b) social security is itself a human right and essential to the realisation of other human rights,*

The challenge was to understand how and where these two types of specification are created, and how they are overseen.

First iteration - reading legislation with a functional eye

All 3 Acts and 76 Ministerial Orders about Scottish Social Security since 2018 were analysed. Each top level section was categorised[20] as follows:

Type	Number	Percentage
Not specification	725	63.1%
Functional Specification	419	36.5%
Non-functional & infrastructural specification	5	0.4%

The evidence is unambiguous - the legislative process specifies the functionality of state computer systems, but doesn't specify the non-functional or infrastructure requirements.

Second iteration - looking for non-functional specifications

Without non-functional & infrastructural specifications there would be no state computer systems, so clearly these decisions are being made somewhere. Investigation shows they are being made everywhere.

One place they are made is the department. Sometimes the right place for non-functional & infrastructural decisions is the implementation team - if you already use technologies X, Y and Z, then choosing them for your new project is a no-brainer.

There are a range of published standards, Scottish government ones, GDS ones, that teams are expected to follow - but the enforcement mechanisms for standards adherence are weak to non-existent. Moral exhortation and leadership by example will only get you so far. Standards are created on a best-endeavours basis by a team or department,

---

20 Figures from Working Paper 9.1

preached across the public sector and taken up unevenly. Compliance of charisma-enforced standards drops off as people move on, reorganisations happen.

Some standards are statutory: accessibility guidelines, General Data Protection Regulations (GDPR) compliance for instance.

There are a number of infrastructure projects at both a UK and Scottish level (payments rails, single-sign-on etc) that are designed to be used across the public sector. The weakness of non-functional & infrastructural decision-making is shown clearly by the fact that these projects are expected to shop themselves around to get uptake.

THIRD ITERATION - OVERSIGHT OF NON-FUNCTIONAL & INFRASTRUCTURAL PROJECTS

The oversight problem is clear. The functional spec is contained in legislation with a functional name - the Social Security (Scotland) Act 2018. That was introduced by a Minister with a functional name - the Cabinet Secretary for Social Security, who sits over a functionally-named department and is overseen by a functionally-named committee of the parliament which takes the functional legislation as its starting point.

Further confirmation of the lack of oversight can be found by a close reading of the *Programme For Government* in which the non-functional & infrastructural elements of the digital state get scant mention. This can be found in Working Paper 9.1 *Reading legislation with a non-functional eye.*

This misbalance - with strong lines of accountability for functional requirements and weak ones for non-functional & infrastructural ones is why state systems are siloed. They have been specified and built in silos. And substantially they should be. The departments and their functions have their own missions, characteristics and cultures and are organic institutions. The challenge is not to replace silos with a giant central monolith, but to build siloed systems with integration points, which expose data and processes such that they can be integrated with other systems. That is fundamentally a design process. It would be mistake to think that purely non-functional specifications can fix that tho. The underlying data in systems, and its processing, is constrained by powers. Civil servants can only do, what they can legally do. Joined up government consists of systems that are both technically and legally capable of being joined up.

At this point, looking across the entire public sector the fundamental philosophical difference between these two types of specification became clear.

Functional specifications have one distinct profile:

Published	Examples	Enforcement
in primary and secondary legislation	Social security Tax Health records Planning etc	The courts
as regulations created under general powers	a vast range of diverse activities	The courts

But non-functional & infrastructural specifications come from a variety of sources:

Published	Examples	Enforcement
in departments	Telephony Workflow/case management Joined up government Data sharing etc	Departmental management
as infrastructure	Sign-ons Payment platforms etc	Best endeavours
on government websites	Design standards Data standards APIs etc	Charisma, leadership
as legislation	GDPR Accessability etc	The courts
as command and control directives	Cybersecurity Cloud-deployment etc	Centralism

These table are indicative and not intended to be comprehensive.

Fourth iteration - review of existing recommendations

The realisation of the importance of the two types of specification came fairly late in the research process when a large number of working papers had been written and the foundation for the majority of recommendations in this report had been sketched out. It should be remembered that the main thrust of the recommendations come from the interviewees experience.

Only one part of one working paper (Working Paper 2

Rules as code) concerns functional matters. And that spawned the only unambiguously functional recommendation[21] in this report. A majority of issues in state computer systems come from the non-functional or infrastructural side.

Fifth iteration - seeking evidence of failure to manage non-functional & infrastructural issues

During his interview the former MSP Andy Wightman brought up *ScotLIS 3 - a critical tool for Scotland: Scotland's land information service: what it is and why it matters*[22] which he wrote for the David Hume Institute on the failures of an integrated land system.

This was a case where there had been unambiguous statements about non-functional & infrastructural requirements at a senior level. Nobody was in any doubt that land data should be delivered in an integrated fashion with a common mapping interface. But the current government institutions and processes where unable to enforce compliance with that and land registers remain unjoined. This is discussed in more detail in Appendix 4 - *Failure to manage non-functionals/infrastructurals in the public sector*.

Sixth iteration - the vexed question of Estonia

Estonia is a paradox. It is the world leading digital state, but lacks a theory of state, there is no Estonian model to copy. This is not that unusual in states that have a first mover

---

21 Recommendation 6.7 - run the strategic research programme and commission new research covers 7 research projects - Property-based testing is functional in nature

22 https://static1.squarespace.com/static/59b82ed532601e01a494df34/t/64075b6d50ab33464b4bfbf6/1678203757948/SCOTLIS+Report+by+Andy+Wightman+March+2023.pdf

advantage.

A minister or politician asking *buy me an Estonia* is a civil service cliché. Everybody knows what 'an Estonia' is, but nobody can articulate why and how Estonia is Estonia.

Estonia has an overarching non-functional requirement that is shared by the government and opposition, by ministers and civil servants, and it is *when the Russians come*.

When the Russians come the entire Estonian administrative estate has to float off and across the border into a government in exile: property registers, electoral register, company registers, citizenship, culture, art, history, elections, taxes, everything.

A library system must meet the functional requirements (lend physical books, lend e-books, track non-returns) and the non-functional one (continue to work and support Estonia as a cultural nation in exile when the Russians come).

A shared overarching non-functional requirement appears to have rebalanced the Estonian state enough to make it work in a fundamentally different way to others.

And it explains in part why the Estonian digital revolution shows signs of having stalled[23] - without a theory of state how do you proceed?

Conclusion

In the analogue age the state created systems with what we can anachronistically call functional and non-functional & infrastructural requirements.

These were decoupled. The infrastructure was buildings

---

23 https://www.ucl.ac.uk/bartlett/public-purpose/sites/public-purpose/files/iipp-wp-2018-09_estonias_digital_transformation.pdf.

with canteens, roofs and windows. The functionality was forms and calculations.

The digital age has new non-functional & infrastructural requirements that are implemented in software and tightly coupled with the functional requirements.

The institutions and structure of laws and government haven't caught up with that shift.

The residuum

A wide range of other issues were chased down, some of which are reflected in the recommendations of this report or expressed as research projects in that part of the recommendations.

Rather than re-litigate them here, the reader is pointed to the Working Papers which contain the relevant detailed discussions:

WP X	*The heart of the beast*
WP 0.3	*The locus of change*
WP 1.2	*Data and the rule of law*
WP 2	*Rules as code*
WP 3	*The Lego state*
WP 4	*The remixable state*
WP 5.1	*Law reform for data*
WP 6	*A solera for data cleansing*
WP 7.3	*Experimental digital legislative processes*
WP 8	*An Enabling Act*
WP 9.1	*Reading legislation with a non-functional eye*
WP 10.2	*Immediate hygienic measures*
WP 11.1	*Jeff Bezos' API mandate, but for Government*

WP 12 *A Theory of State*

WP 13 *The weak centre*

The conclusions

The conclusions can be summarised in three paragraphs:

The government needs a single organisation with the mechanism to make decisions about **how** *digital systems should work, and parliament needs a single structure to oversee those decisions.*

Decisions about **what** *digital systems should do are made sub-optimally by parliament using ad-hoc repurposed mechanisms.*

The state lacks a research capability for digital systems.

ABSENCE OF EVIDENCE

There was no evidence of a skills gap, of methodologies and approaches that that private sector tech companies have but civil servants don't. Civil servants are less effective in the digital arena than their private sector comparators because of structural and systemic sequencing and process issues - which this report addresses.

There *appears* to be a major skills gap between senior executives of major tech companies and the political class that oversees what is by any reasonable measure a major internet estate.

But overseeing digital systems and services is only one of many, many critical jobs that the political class has to do and this seemingly damaging indictment is glib and superficial.

Oversight and management of the digital state is a

constitutional and institutional matter and its excellence will not be found in this person or that.

Institutionalising best practice

All the things required for the management of both functional and non-functional & infrastructural requirements are known, discovered and documented. The standards that we need to build new ways of working have already been written.

The absence of an institutional foundation makes itself felt in a variety of ways. There are standards from different parts of the state that overlap and contradict each other. There are standards that have fallen in desuetude and need to be reinvented and rewritten. There are standards that are not being maintained and updated.

The challenge is to build constitutionally appropriate institutions to put this existing work on a proper institutional basis. Those institutions must respect the very real constraints on parliament.

CHAPTER SIX

Issues in designing the new system

Introduction

There is no blank sheet in planning new ways of working - the future is always constrained by the present.

Before proceeding to talk about detailed recommendations it is necessary to outline the constraints that were imposed on the design.

A focus of this work has been *Constitutionnalité* - proper forms. The digital age has brought old problems in new bottles and where ever possible precedents for proposed structures and processes have been sought.

Constraints

The constraints are few, but hard.

Government activities need parliamentary oversight - the separation of powers must be respected.

The throughput of the parliament is limited: 20-25 Acts and 400-450 Ministerial Orders a year. The proposals must not overwhelm parliament with additional work.

Parliament has other jobs than supervising the digital state. Bills derived from Scottish Law Commission reports currently take 5% to 10% of its time. Legislative proposals from this report should certainly be within that limit.

Precedents

A range of precedents were considered for:

- New institutions
- The handling of non-functional & infrastructural requirements

New institutions

Institutional precedents were sought in:

- the taming of atomic technologies
- separation of powers in the Scottish parliament
- the oversight of Social Security at Westminster and Holyrood
- Ontario Digital Services and the Simpler, Faster, Better Services Act

These precedents are discussed in Working Paper 0.3 *The locus of change*.

The handling of non-functional & infrastructural requirements

Precedents were sought in:

- web governance and internet standards
- the Amazon API Mandate and the transformation of Amazon from a retailer to a provider of services and platforms
- the history of the bill pack and the financial resolution

These precedents are discussed in:

- Working Paper 0.3 *The locus of change*
- Working Paper 10.2 Immediate hygienic measures
- Working Paper 11.1 *Jeff Bezos' API Mandate, but for government*

CHAPTER SEVEN
Final comments

Final comments

The process followed has been methodical and practitioner-led. Problems have been chased down recursively with a view to identifying root causes. Care has been taken to ensure that the recommendations are both constitutional and achievable within the constraints of the existing systems.

The report goes where the evidence took it. A measure of that journey can be seen by comparing the final recommendations and system design to the original research hypotheses of Appendix 2 - *Digital Fellowship research axioms and hypotheses*.

PART THREE

SYSTEM DESIGN AND RECOMMENDATIONS

CHAPTER EIGHT

Introduction to the proposed system design and detailed recommendations

Introduction

This project is at its core a systematisation project and only has innovation in systems design.

There is an inherent tension in how to present the results. On the one hand the principle of *Explicite* says we need to show the operation of the system in the round, from start to finish. On the other hand, people have specific jobs, in one part of the system. It behooves us to enable them to understand the impact on them and their daily work directly - the principle of *Simplicité*.

This part will do both. First up is a description of the 3 major themes of system change which will reference individual recommendations:

- unitary specification of services and systems
- better iteration in service development
- developing a research capability

After that the recommendations will be stepped through in detail, following the foundational process cycle described in the methodology.

The legislative enactments are then listed - and finally a phased implementation plan is laid out.

CHAPTER NINE
System view of recommendations

Introduction to the system view of recommendations

The systems design addresses both the how of state digital systems and the what separately. But they are entangled by the institutional design. The core institutions play a critical role in the implementation and must first find themselves and their voice.

BOOTSTRAPPING

Before the major themes of work can begin a certain degree of bootstrapping must be done - simple, quick win tasks that can establish the infrastructure for the major programmes.

Critically these tasks should also demonstrate benefit from Day 1 - establishing credibility early when the team is small is an essential precondition for successful transformation programmes.

THE 3 MAJOR THEMES

Each of these will be discussed separately:

- unitary specification of services and systems
- better iteration in service development
- developing a research capability

Each theme starts with a recapitulation of ***why***? What is the purpose of this work? What is the citizen benefit?

Then the ***issues*** with the current state will be sketched out.

After that ***success*** is defined. How will be know if this project has been successful?

Finally the ***system design*** will be explained.

Bootstrapping

Introduction

There is a core technical team on the government side that will play a critical role in the long term implementation of these recommendations. This team should bootstrap itself with a small set of hygienic measures - things that we are either not doing or doing intermittently that we know we ought to be doing every time.

Purpose

There are two purposes to the bootstrapping activities:

- team building - the final state team needs to be created, needs to bond and find its voice
- quick wins - it is important for major change projects to demonstrate value quickly

There are two things to be bootstrapped, the relationship of the programme of work with:

- the policy community
- the parliament

The policy community

The big thing being changed by all of the 3 major programmes is the relationship between the policy and delivery/technical communities.

There is an annual policy training seminar series in Scottish Government which 200+ civil servants attend. It makes no mention of technology. Neither does the Legislation and Policy Unit's *Bill Handbook*[24]. The nascent DSRO team

---

24 https://www.gov.scot/binaries/content/documents/govscot/publicatio

need to insert themselves into this training and start building relations with the policy teams. There will be a new, prototype Systems Impact Assessment (SIA) which will be mandatory. The finance team offers bill teams dedicated support in writing their Financial Memorandums, the DSRO should adopt that model - *here's new work you have to do, and here is how we will help you do it.*

In this phase the DSRO will just be asking the teams *have you thought about data*? *are you talking to your in-service and delivery teams*?

The parliament

There are two ways in which the new prototype Systems Impact Assessment could be introduced:

- the government could just add it to the pile or create a new section in the Explanatory Notes
- the parliament could change its concept of what Proper Form is and insist on it

Convenience would suggest adopting the first approach, but that would be a mistake. The introduction of a SIA should be on an experimental basis for a selected Bill and reflected in a temporary standing order to mimic the way in which the large changes will be delivered and enable relationships with the parliament to be built and a quick win delivered. The strategic goal is to make the twin elements of the bill text and the SIA a point of unitary specification. The bill text contains the ***what*** and the SIA the ***how***.

---

ns/foi-eir-release/2022/07/foi-202200306018/documents/foi-202200306018---information-released/foi-202200306018---information-released/govscot%3Adocument/FOI%2B202200306018%2B-%2BInformation%2Breleased.pdf

FURTHER DETAILS

Working Paper 10.2 - *Immediate Hygienic Measures* describes bootstrapping in greater detail.

Implementation of bootstrapping

Recommendations

The detailed recommendations that support this are:

6 - *create a Digital Services Reform Office*, including:

- 6.1 - *the foundations of the DSRO*
- 6.2 - *changes to the PLU's Bill Handbook*
- 6.3 - *improved organisational support for the PLU and Bill Teams*

8 - *changes to the Bill Pack, etc*, including:

- 8.1 - *changes to the Bill Pack for primary legislation*
- 8.2 - *changes to the Explanatory Notes for secondary legislation*
- 8.3 - *approvals process for day-to-day services implementation*

These do not require any legislative enactments.

Context for major theme 1 - unitary specification of services and systems

Introduction

At its heart, this stream of work addresses the non-functional & infrastructural problem described in Working Paper 9.1 - *Reading legislation with a non-functional eye*. It is about changing how the state makes decisions about ***how*** digital systems should work.

This part of the report recommends two new institutions.

The first is a government body - the Digital Services Reform Office (DSRO), which has the power to issue standards and recommend both legislative changes and programmes of work.

The DSRO is the technical leadership of the civil service. As such it takes on critical roles in the other two major programmes. It oversees the improvements in iteration and commissions and supervises the research programmes.

The second is a parliamentary body - the Digital Services Scrutiny & Audit Commission (DSS&AC) which also plays an oversight role of the iteration and research programmes.

But both are designed here as a pair of institutions.

Why does this system matter?

This system enables joined-up government and data sharing. It will reduce the amount of time that the citizen, or companies, spend engaging with the state. There will be more data reuse and data will be more up-to-date and coherent. It will reduce rework in digital systems, whether that is building again things that already exist elsewhere, or making alterations to in-service systems. The state will be able to make better use of the data that it already has. Disjoints between different areas of government will be reduced.

What are the problems that it addresses?

This system fixes a major defect in how the state currently works.

State administrative systems in the 1950s had functional and non-functional & infrastructural specifications that were decoupled.

The functional specifications were of the form *administrate social security*, and the non-functional & infrastructural specifications were of the form *have a building*.

With the advent of the digital age this changed. A second set of non-functional & infrastructural specifications were added which were about digital and not physical infrastructure. The implementation of these specifications is of course tightly coupled with that of the functional specification - its all just software.

The evidence[25] is that this transition was not addressed in government processes. Legislation includes the functional specification. The non-functional & infrastructural work is delegated to the departments as it was in the 1950s.

For the non-coupled physical infrastructure this process continues to work. For the coupled digital infrastructure (which includes joined up government and data sharing) departmental delegation fails.

The system replaces departmental infrastructural

---

25 See Working Paper 9.1 Reading legislation with a non-functional eye

specification with a central standards-based approach with a light touch enforcement mechanism.

In 1911 Lloyd George designed the first cut of the GP system. In the 1980s his legislation provided the design of both systems and data for basic GP administration, unintentionally. At the moment departments are making autonomous and unconscious decisions that potentially have a century-long impact. This system will make those decisions explicit, public and subject to parliamentary scrutiny.

How will we know if it successful?

Success will be visible in more effective use of data, more effective joined up government and higher use of common services like sign-ons and payment systems.

Departments will participate in the work of the DSRO and its work will be informed by technical specialists from all parts of the public sector.

Departments have high degrees of operational autonomy.

What does failure look like?

Failure looks like a command and control system that centralises decision making on the DSRO which issues edicts and enforces them.

System design of major theme 1 - unitary specification of services and systems

Introduction to the system design

The twin institutions, the government actor and the parliamentary overseer, need to be designed together as a single system.

The Digital Services Reform Office (DSRO) is the government body, which in its reform proposals rhymes with the Scottish Law Commission. The DSRO has the power to issue standards and recommend both legislative changes and programmes of work. These activities need to be adopted by the government of the day to proceed.

The Digital Services Scrutiny & Audit Commission (DSS&AC) is the parliamentary oversight body. It works under the supervision of a parliamentary committee. In its scrutiny work it rhymes with the Scottish Commission on Social Security and it its audit work it rhymes with Audit Scotland.

There are changes to the form of the Bill Pack that enable the unitary specification of services and systems. When the Minister introduces a Bill in Parliament the functional requirements will be covered in the Bill text and the non-functional & infrastructural requirements will be in a new Systems Impact Assessment (SIA). Where the DSRO has published standards and guidelines appropriate to the system under discussion, the SIA will reference them.

Civil servants in the technical trades will have two lines of responsibility, to their departmental minister for functionality and to the parliament via the DSRO and DSS&AC

for infrastructure.

The principle of this two part design is *Constitutionnalité* - the separation of powers.

The Digital Services Reform Office

The structure and powers of the DRSO are based on the Scottish Law Commission – although there are significant differences.

The DSRO is staffed by career civil servants from the technical trades and can be considered to be the professional apex of those trades.[26] There will be 3 core statutory technical positions:

- Government Design Officer (GDeO)
- Government Technology Officer (GTO)
- Government Data Officer (GDaO)

In their work they are supported by an advisory board of technical experts from the private sector and academia. The DSRO sits directly under the Permanent Secretary and will be chaired by the Chief Digital Officer. Its mission is to drive the capability of the state and the core mechanism for doing that is the issuing of technical standards. Standards have the power of co-ordination without communication. Technical standards and standard-making bodies underpin the internet, and the DSRO rhymes with internet organisations in its processes.

The staff members of the DSRO will be statutory persons with a requirement to be answerable to parliament - via the DSS&AC. This line of responsibility mirrors that of Senior Accounting Officers and Senior Responsible Owners. As an

---

26 *Pace* Hutton, Fulton and Maude

institution the DSRO will have a right of audience at both the Holyrood and Westminster parliaments.

The work of the DSRO will only touch parliament occasionally, the bulk of it will not be primary or secondary legislation - therefore the DSRO will have an obligation to lay a report covering all its work before the parliament each year.

It will be able to draw up plans of work, have the power to lay them before Parliament (unamended by the government of the day), and recommend changes to primary and secondary legislation. However the implementation of those plans requires the assent of Ministers.

The experience of the Ontario Digital Services was that about 100 pieces of legislation needed changing to sand off rough edges that prevented digitisation. An Enabling Act will be enacted so that Parliament is not overwhelmed. The operation of that Act will be under the supervision of the DSS&AC in the first instance.

The DSRO has 3 roles in unitary specification[27]:

- it creates and issues technical standards. This rhymes with the technical standards body of the internet the IETF/W3C
- it commissions and oversee central services that are required to support a standards and components-based regime. This rhymes with the central infrastructure function of the internet ICANN
- it manages the development of tooling shared across the Scottish public sector and with other jurisdictions around the world. Tooling (or embedding technical

[27] The DSRO has additional roles under the other major work streams

standards into code libraries and infrastructure) is the way in which standards-compliance is made easy. This rhymes with the various bodies supporting open source infrastructural software like the Mozilla and Apache Foundations

A more detailed discussion of the DSRO can be found in Working Paper 0.3 *The locus of change* which looks at the capabilities it needs to support, its structure and powers, and the precedents for them and the proposed changes to parliamentary process. This discussion includes the differences between the structure and powers of the DSRO and those of the Scottish Law Commission.

Working Paper 8 *An Enabling Act* discusses how to enable legislative changes whilst protecting the rule of law and providing adequate scrutiny.

Working Paper 11.1 *Jeff Bezos' Memo, but for government* drafts an initial charter for the DSRO based on the pivotal non-functional & infrastructural directive that changed Amazon from a bookseller to a provider of cloud services.

Working Paper 12 *A theory of state* outlines a theory of state for the design of unitary specification.

Working Paper 13 *A weak centre* puts the case for strong departments and against centralisation.

The Digital Services Scrutiny & Audit Commission

The DSS&AC is the child of a new parliamentary committee and acts on behalf of that committee, triaging issues and escalating problems to it.

The DSS&AC has two functions:

- it scrutinises standards and proposed legislation coming from the DSRO on behalf of its parent

committee as a first line of accountability
- it audits compliance of departments with the standards and guidelines

The membership of the DSS&AC will be:

- technical specialists
- social scientists
- ethicists
- legal experts

Its job is to scrutinise the desirability as well as the feasibility of technical proposals.

A more detailed discussion of the DSRO can be found in Working Paper 0.3 *The locus of change* which discusses its precedents, powers and membership.

Changes to Parliamentary Procedure

The point of unitary specification is the Bill Pack. The format of the Bill Pack is not within the gift of government, it is the clerks of Parliament who determine if a Bill is in proper form on submission.

Both the proposals here and the implementation plan must conform to *Constitutionnalité* and so the implementation plan must be a joint process between government and parliament conducted not as politics as usual, but on the constitutional plane.

Changes to the Role of Civil Servants

A small number of civil servants currently have dual lines of responsibility to parliament and their minister. That number will increase appropriately.

Implementation of major theme 1 - unitary specification of services and systems

Recommendations

The detailed recommendations that support this are:

6 - *create a Digital Services Reform Office*, including:

- 6.1 - *the foundations of the DSRO*

8 - *changes to the Bill Pack, etc*, including:

- 8.1 - *changes to the Bill Pack for primary legislation*
- 8.2 - *changes to the Explanatory Notes for secondary legislation*
- 8.3 - *approvals process for day-to-day services implementation*

10 - *create a Digital Services Scrutiny & Audit Commission*

15 - *changes to lines of responsibility in the civil service*

Legislative enactments

These changes require the following legislative enactments:

1 - *putting the DSRO on a statutory basis*

2 - *putting the DSS&AC on a statutory basis*

The legislative burden of unitary specification is estimated to be the approximately that of the Scottish Law Commission. Law reform currently takes one to two bills a year, or between 5% and 10% of parliamentary capacity.

Context for major theme 2 - better iteration in service development

INTRODUCTION

Delivering software systems is not like delivering roads or bridges. Physical infrastructure is ***complicated*** but you can work up a detailed plan up front and execute on it. Digital systems are ***complex*** because they work with people. When you drop them into a society they start changing people. Behaviours, culture and organisations mould themselves to them. Digital systems are also deeply opaque and hard to reason about.

Nearly 30 years into the mass internet age we know that major software development should be done iteratively. Prototypes should be built as early as possible so that developers can see users using them, and those commissioning the systems know what is being built.

The challenge is to find ways to preserve the constitutional architecture - *the government proposes, the parliament disposes* - whilst increasing the speed of iteration.

WHY DOES THIS SYSTEM MATTER?

This is a roadmap for better government in the digital age. There is no area of government that doesn't build on digital foundations. The design, development and maintenance of those foundations is of critical interest to anyone who cares about state capability. The digital age promises better services, lower costs, more responsive government, these changes deliver that.

WHAT ARE THE PROBLEMS THAT IT ADDRESSES?

The fundamental problem this theme tries is to address is that legislative process freezes iteration. Law is as iterative as software development, but on a longer cycle.

Fundamentally the quicker you can execute an iterative cycle, the quicker you can spot and fix problems and change direction.

The simplest analogy is driving a car - that is a process of continuous and smooth adjustments of the steering wheel. What would it look like if there was an enforced rhythm to that - you could only move the steering wheel every half second, second, minute, hour, day? The legislative process brings long pauses between adjusting the steering wheel.

This theme begins to address that by driving as much of the journey before the legislative steering damper kicks in. Building software prototypes that people can use, building paper prototypes, testing policy and implementation with actual citizens. As much of this work as is practically possible should be done before embarking on primary or secondary legislation.

HOW WILL WE KNOW IF IT SUCCESSFUL?

Iterative speed is a measurable quantity.

System design of major theme 2 - better iteration in service development

INTRODUCTION TO THE SYSTEM DESIGN

This involves moving a range of design and testing activities earlier in the overall specification process.

But better iteration also requires moving service delivery fundamentally in the political space, from a 2nd class consideration to a 1st class one.

And therefore it affects government, parliament and civic society.

THE GOVERNMENT SIDE

On the government side there is a slew of recommendations that affect the operation of the policy community and the integration of policy and delivery (for areas where there are substantial digital foundations). The DSRO has a strategic role in guiding digital policy development and ensuring that best practices, including iteration, are built into daily working processes. These activities will make non-functional & infrastructural issues more visible in the *Programme for Government* and more amenable to scrutiny.

THE PARLIAMENTARY SIDE

On the parliamentary side there is increased support for MSPs in general, and the opposition in particular.

These proposals do not aim to turn MSPs into boffins. MSPs and the parliamentary parties do not operate in isolation and are embedded in the wider world of constituents, the extra-parliamentary party, think tanks and interest groups of all kinds. The goal here is to drive greater understanding outside parliament and help elected members shape and channel that understanding politically.

There is a second phase to better iteration for the parliamentary side too. It is to be found in the research programme in Recommendation 11 - *a review of legislative processes for major digital programmes*. This review looks at legislation as an iterative process in light of the evidence presented in Working Paper 9.1 *Reading legislation with a non-functional eye*.

There is no doubt that for major digital systems like social security, the functional requirements are developed and delivered iteratively. However the iterative process is undesigned, repurposes existing structural instruments of secondary legislation and is sub-optimal.

Changes to legislative processes again are substantially constitutional in nature and need to approached in cross-party manner with co-working between parliament and government.

There are no major digital programmes of the scale of Social Security on the immediate horizon, but there will be on a hundred year horizon. There is time to do the work and address the legislative iteration issues patiently, methodically and in-depth.

Government and parliament

This report focuses on process to ensure that:

- decision makers take decisions they are qualified to do, whether ministers or parliamentarians
- the best information is available to decision makers
- expert input into decision making is appropriately scrutinised
- the right considerations have been taken into account
- the right experts and citizens affected have been consulted
- all consultations have been as effective as possible
- assumptions have been tested as thoroughly as possible

In addition technical decision-making needs to be separated out, with steps taken to ensure that Ministers and Parliament have confidence in the quality of it by putting in place expert scrutiny.

The principle of *Constitutionnalité* pertains. Better opposition occasions better government.

Civic society

For civic society, journalism and think tanks there are changes to publication requirements to present more appropriate information about digital systems that will enable more questioning of the government's strategy and delivery and increase political pressure.

These publication and audit changes reflect the split between functional requirements (***what*** things are done) and non-functional & infrastructural (***how*** things are done). We publish a lot of operational data - which by its nature reflects the internal view of ***what*** things are done - waiting lists, exam results, the processing of applications. In addition to this we need to have a holistic view of ***how*** things are done.

This splits into two. There is operational non-functional & infrastructural data. An example would be what proportion of government payments are made through the strategic payments system. But there also needs to be external surveyed data about citizens experience of digital systems - which is non-operational.

There are fundamental problems with over-relying on operational data and fetishising real-time data. It fundamentally represents a limited view of the world, and the experience of the in-service organisation. To understand this, it is best to consider crime figures. The police collate and publish crime figures as reported to them. The citizen's experience of crime is caught in the Scottish Crime and Justice Survey. These figures are complementary but not congruent.

Driving political pressure requires more non-functional & infrastructural data on all fronts - and balancing data in both forms. Much of operational management in the private sector is taken up with attempting to understand and reconcile contradictory data signals - government and politics is no different. These elements are *Explicite* in action.

Implementation of major theme 2 - better iteration in service development

RECOMMENDATIONS

The detailed recommendations that support this are:

1 - *an obligation to publish non-functional & infrastructural statistics about state operations*

2 - *Registers of Services, Powers and Policies*

3 - *widening access to data*

4 - *widening access to research fellowships*

5 - *Short money considerations*

6 - *create a Digital Services Reform Office*, including:

- 6.2 - *changes to the PLU's Bill Handbook*
- 6.3 - *improved organisational support for the PLU and Bill Teams*
- 6.4 - *make non-functional & infrastructural work visible in the Programme for Government*
- 6.6 - *the development and proposition of machinery of government changes*

- 6.9 - *a user-centred design roadshow*
- 6.10 - *an information architecture*

12 - *publication of legislative amendments*

13 - *additional capabilities for SPICe*

14 - *testing needs to be made a first class professional discipline in Government*

Legislative enactments

These changes require the following legislative enactments:

3 - *an Enabling Act*

4 - *new register of services*

5 - *new register of powers*

6 - *new register of policy*

7 - *amendments to The Interpretation And Legislative Reform (Scotland) Act 2011*

8 - *obligation to release data*

9 – *obligation to publish non-functional & infrastructural statistics*

10 - *a Data Bill of Rights*

Context for major theme 3 - developing a research capability

Introduction

This is in some ways an extension of the previous theme on iteration. It moves the experimentation phase back even further - *what sort of policy could we do if we had what sort of technology available?*

Why does this system matter?

The best way to predict the future is to invent it - and at the moment Scotland isn't inventing the future of government. Research is the mother of invention.

This proposal covers both specific invention-of-the-future proposals building on this research and a standing institutional capability built on the foundations of our existing innovative technology organisation - CivTech.

What are the problems that it addresses?

There are four related problems.

1. Due to time and resource pressures, this report failed to do local government and other sub-state bodies justice. One of the research proposals is to complete that part of the original mission.
2. The state does not currently have the capability to execute the law reform process outlined in more detail in Working Paper 5.1 *Law reform for data*. The problem can be articulated but not resolved at this point.
3. There is no doubt that there is a need to redesign legislative processes for iteration is. That work can only be done in a constitutional fashion by people with an appropriate political and organisational mandate. This is discussed in Working Paper 7.3 *Experimental digital legislative processes*.
4. CivTech has been incrementally growing in maturity, this recommendation completes that journey.

How will we know if it successful?

Fundamentally, like all research, there will be a failure rate. The goal of the design is to contain the research costs, do the projects under constrained sprints and assess viability and value as early as possible. This aspect of the recommendations will be successful if the scale and ambition of technology use in the state increases significantly.

System design of major theme 3 - developing a research capability

Three of these proposals have no system design beyond *do them*! The seven CivTech proposals do.

We can map the history of CivTech's innovation onto our process cycle:

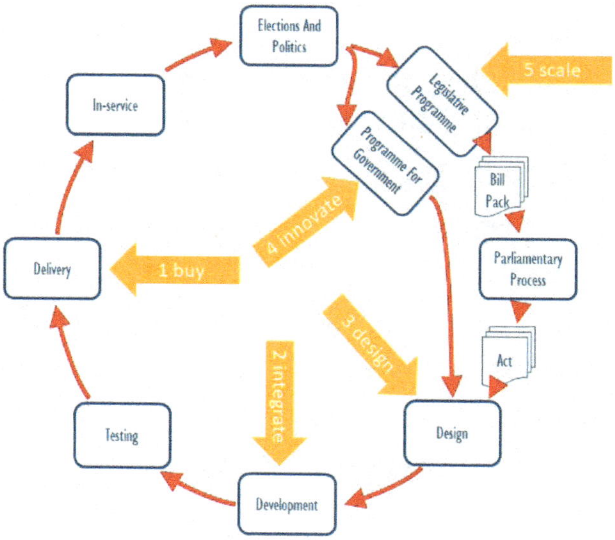

In caricature, CivTech went through this evolution:

1 a procurement arm - buy to fit

2 an integrator of new technology into GovTech

3 an enabler of better design of tech solutions

4 a tech innovator (but only on 3rd channel policies - that is to say policy that is day-to-day and not implemented in

primary or secondary legislation)

The final stage is becoming an innovator at scale. It would do the R&D for major system proposals that could be as important as Scottish Social Security.

Working Paper 3 *The Lego state* and Working Paper 4 *The remixable state* are both proposals with impact at that scale.[28]

These and other possible pieces of work that currently are beyond the grasp of the Scottish state have been identified and CivTech should commission and stand-up small team (3-5) bounded research spikes in these areas with the view to producing working prototypes, procedures, training packs or change programmes.

The teams in this R&D process would consist of civil servants (policy, design and technology) augmented by external contractors with specialist skills if appropriate.

Prototypes, working systems and MVPs that capture the essence of strategic possibilities, no matter how simple, are enormously powerful.

Policy makers, senior leadership, lawyers, ministers and parliamentarians can participate in discussions on a more equal basis with a tangible expression of innovation in front of them. Show beats tell every time.

There would be two other significant side effect - a cadre of civil servants with hands-on experience of integrated policy/tech iterative design and development. On rotating back to their previous roles, they would apply that thinking to other policies, problems, issues and opportunities.

And the research programme should actively proselytise

---

28 At the systems scale of Social Security Scotland, not at it's money-out-of-the-door scale

new ways and possibilities around ministers, the parliament and civil society. It should be the shop window of the possible.

As the DSRO builds itself up, it should commission R&D projects from CivTech under its own recognisances. The list in this report is just a pump primer.

There are seven research proposals - four of them under the general rubric of Rules As Code.

Rules as Code aims to bring computational discipline to rule-making, particularly to rules in legislation.

It is a broad field. For the purpose of this report, it is the technique of annotating legislation such that the annotations can be machine compiled into executable code. For an overview please see Working Paper 2 *Rules as code.*

The seven identified potential CivTech-led research projects are:

- generating MVPs from legislation using Rules As Code
- generating components for macro-economic modelling from tax legislation using Rules As Code
- property-based testing to slash major project management overheads for substantial calculation-intensive major programme software development (social security or taxation) using Rules As Code
- reducing barriers to entry into regulated industries by creating model implementations of regulatory systems using Rules as Code
- developing methodologies and processes for component design, promotion and publication (see Working Paper 3 *The lego state*)
- exploring delegated authority as a core structural

model for remixability and refocus (see Working Paper 4 *The remixable state*)

- revisiting on-prem and global scale capacity

A summary of these projects can be found in Appendix 5 - *CivTech Research Proposals.*

This list of CivTech research projects are ones arising from my research, which must be a partial view. It is appropriate that when the DSRO sets itself up, it canvasses widely on the subject of possible research projects and draws up its own list, which may or may not include these seven

These research projects address problems that are not unique to Scotland. Other governments should be approached to participate.

In addition there are three major research projects not suitable for CivTech.

Implementation of major theme 3 - developing a research capability

The CivTech research is covered by:

6.7 - *run the strategic research programme and commission new research*

The CivTech research programmes feed into:

6.9 - *a user-centred design roadshow*

There are two additional research projects that are required, but which are not suitable for short CivTech programmes as they are less technical and more process-based and have constitutional and legal implications. They covered by the recommendations:

6.5 - *a law reform process for data*

6.8 - *participation in a joint review of legislative processes with the parliament*

11 - *a review of legislative processes for major digital programmes*

The last two are the two halves of a joint programme.

These research proposals do not require legislation up front - but their outputs will require using other legislative enactments already proposed:

3 - *an Enabling Act*

4 - *new register of services*

5 - *new register of powers*

Recommendation 11 may also require technical changes to Section 36[29] of the Scotland Act 1998.

Due to pressures of time, this research project was unable to give local government and health boards appropriate consideration and the final recommendation proposes a research project to address this:

7 - *review the process of creating legislation for local government and other sub-state bodies*

---

[29] https://www.legislation.gov.uk/ukpga/1998/46/section/36

CHAPTER TEN

Process view of recommendations

Introduction

This section looks at concrete and detailed recommendations.

They form a complex mechanism. Building out this should be done incrementally. This involves a development cycle of a simple implementation followed by use/review/adjust cycles before becoming their final form. That might be on a statutory or standards-specified basis.

On first blush this report appears legislation heavy. The proposing 10 enactments can be consolidated to 2 or 3 Acts over 3 to 5 years.

The enactments themselves are not that extensive. The great mass of details will come from two things:

- technical standards that will emerge from the new institutions
- Ministerial Orders via the Enabling Act

The experience of Ontario was that 100 Acts had to be amended in digitisation. The law reform proposal here would increase that - and this work would be done under the proposed Enabling Act.

It should also be remembered that these recommendations apply only to a fragment of the work of parliament and government. The vast majority of the work of both will not be affected by them at all.

The recommendations will be discussed in the context of the development cycle:

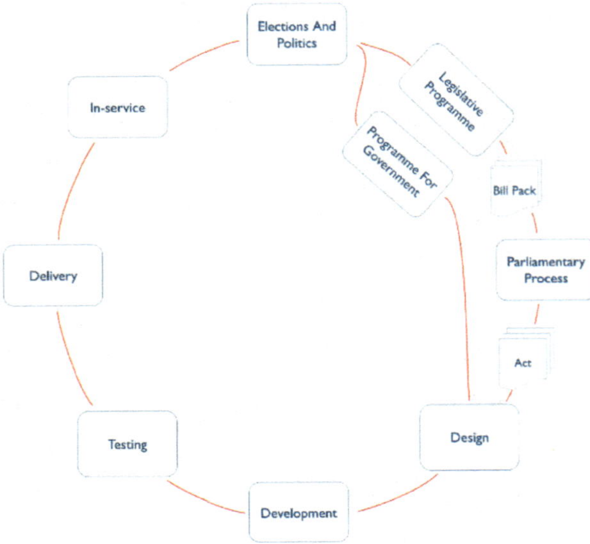

	Stage	No
1	In-service	2
2	Elections and politics	3
3	Government institutions and the programme for government (including the legislative and non-legislative elements)	11
4	The bill pack, etc	3
5	Parliamentary institutions and processes	4
6	Testing	1
7	Delivery	1

THE NATURE OF THESE RECOMMENDATIONS

These recommendations are fundamentally conservative - the innovation is in the whole, the system.

There are no recommendations for the design of services and systems and the development of software, and testing and delivery get a minor recommendation apiece.

Fundamentally this report can be summarised as *take holistic design and delivery more seriously and consider their core elements earlier before law or code is cut* and having done that *put in place procedures and oversight to ensure that it happens*.

The non-functional & infrastructural work is a key part of the holistic design.

The conservatism flows from the methodology: asking practitioners about their work and their discontents.

But the systems innovation profoundly breaches some deeply ingrained taboos.

To civil servants the pre-legislative political arena is a third rail - touch at your peril. But the political arena directs, shapes and drives political pressure, and that pressure, in turn and in part, changes how the civil service dances.

And the parliament guards its privileges well, it is of the state but not the government and a forbidden land for the civil service.

The technical trades in the civil service have bubbled with innovation over the last 15 years - but that innovation has been constrained and contained by the twin taboos leading to a certain inarticulacy on political and constitutional matters.

Politicians and ministers are the overseers of civil servants in one sense, the matter of *policy intent*. But they are merely peers of them in matters of *policy effect* - co-equal participants in a development cycle. They get to choose the direction but not to specify the tasks and the sequence they must be executed in.

This report largely is the institutionalising of operational innovation by the technical trades over the last decade - and pushing back obligations onto the political classes.

Technical inarticulacy has been matched on the political side by a lack of operational thinking.

The long battle within the civil service has been christological - are the two natures (policy and delivery) united in one body (the team) or are they separate and distinct?

This report is on the winning side - unity of policy and delivery.

On the political side the war has (sometimes) gone the other way. In some parts of UK politics, policy has become detached, free floating, phantasmagorical, unmoored.

This is partly structural and therefore addressable in this report.

Included in the interviewees were manifesto writers from the SNP, Labour and the Conservatives, for UK and Scottish elections alike.

There was cross-party unanimity on one issue. Manifestos are split between defensive content (tax and spending) and retail offerings to citizens.

Tax and spending is on the defensive side because there is an institutional infrastructure of audit and publication that generates academic and civil society scrutiny which in turn feeds journalism and opinion, and onto political pressure.

The digital state features in manifestos on the retail side as *we will rub some flavour of the month tech on government to make it better*. The flavour has changed from time - from e-Government, web sites, apps, blockchain to the current hot button AI.

The switch from an analogue to a digital state is a profound change.

Shifting that capability from being motherhood'n'apple pie retail politics to defensive, hard question politics is a critical, and institutional question.

These factors are also reflected in the nature of this report and analysis which is profoundly operational, concerned with capability and steeped in delivery. By contrast traditional public sector reform programmes are policy- and outcome-focussed.

Introduction to in-service recommendations

The transition from analogue to digital state hinges on the institutional treatment of non-functional & infrastructural issues. This can be seen in the information that is published about the state.

Firstly the information is skewed to the functional - waiting times, exam league tables - and away from the non-functionals & infrastructurals - can you use state websites? how do you navigate multiple systems? how many times must you enter the same data? how often do you inform multiple bodies of one change of circumstance?

Key programmes - the aqueducts and reservoirs of digital infrastructure - are practically invisible.

Secondly the information is incomplete - hot button/high volume services are visible, but lots are not.

Registers of services, publication standards and other core audit operations are not institutionalised. Political pressure is a response to what can be seen.

If your department is not 'hot' and there is no real focus on it, then there is no pressure to ensure that your websites are usable or that you make public dashboards and operational information that could inform the public.

In fact there is the risk that if you are open, you will create political pressure, bring the spotlight.

The private sector must seduced with honeyed words, and a poor user experience is rewarded with bankruptcy. The public sector can compel with bayonets. If poor user experience isn't turned into political heat, it will never be fixed.

Recommendation 1 - an obligation to publish non-functional & infrastructural statistics about state operations

Description

This recommendation is the rebalancing of official statistics from being dominated by functional considerations and bringing hidden elements of state capability into the light.

It falls into two parts:

- The visible - services exposed to citizens directly, eg shared digital identity

- The invisible - back-end processes exposed as services to other citizen facing-systems, eg state payment systems

Almost all web-based systems have internal facing dashboards that show the core statistics:

- usage volumes
- user paths
- completion
- funnel behaviour and customer behaviour

(This functionality is baked into most web frameworks.)

The dashboards might also show other core metrics:

- cost per transaction
- user satisfaction/Net Promoter Score (NPS)

This basic information should be part of the publication obligation. Non-functional & infrastructural operational data should be also mirrored with external survey data.

Institutional basis

This recommendation is under the supervision of the DSS&AC which defines the audit standards and performs the appropriate audit.

Legislation Required 9 – *obligation to publish non-functional & infrastructural statistics*

Development

Departments should maintain their own dashboards - which will be public. A link to the dashboard will be an obligatory part of the registration in the Register of Services - see Recommendation 2.

This will initially be an informal requirement, but as the

standardisation process continues it should become statutory.

Recommendation 2 - Registers of Services, Powers and Policies

Description

There is no single register of services that the state provides - without this key base information it is not possible to build any sort of stable communities of interest in the wider political world. The same goes for powers under which systems are developed, and policies that are in operation

The goal here is to have a simple, legally required register of services where different government departments and public bodies manage their entries themselves (think a simpler version of Companies House but for government services).

State bodies will be obliged to register their services and maintain their register entry which will include its URL space.[30] When a service is closed down it will be so marked. The register will be human and machine readable and slight, with much of its content link-backs to the registered service.

A comprehensive register is a critical single source of truth. Around it details of the cost, performance, consumption of citizen and organisational time of state systems can be

---

30 URLs, Uniform Resource Locators include things like web addresses. The URL system is a uniform global name space. The way in which domain names (which core elements of URLs) are delegated means that domain owners can sub-delegate and by using wild cards that match delegated authority we can capture the URL space a service 'owns' eg *.myservice.gov.scot/*

aggregated.

Knowing these basic things is the foundation of digital transformation:

> *At the moment we do this, it costs this, if we make this change we could do that and it would save this much time and this much money.*

As the standards kick in and we move to a more mature world, systems will start being self-reporting with tooling built in that published data schemas, change logs, etc, etc. That information won't be copied onto the central register which will be kept simple, but connected via link-backs.

Similarly with the other proposed institutional registers - the register of powers and the register of policies. The register of policies would be self-service, but the register of powers emerges from consideration of legislation.

INSTITUTIONAL BASIS

This register will be of a form defined in statute in an amendment to the Interpretation And Legislative Reform (Scotland) Act (2010).[31]

Legislation Required 4 - *new register of services*

Legislation Required 7 - *amendments to The Interpretation And Legislative Reform (Scotland) Act 2011*

The formal contents of the register will be a standard issued by the DSRO.

DEVELOPMENT

The first versions of this register will be a simple website maintained by the DSRO. Aggressive *de minimis* (100,000

---

31 https://www.legislation.gov.uk/asp/2010/10/contents

users, 1,000,000 transactions a year, etc, etc) will be used to keep the number of systems required to register small to start with. Over time those limits will be reduced to bring more systems in scope.

After it has matured the register will be put on a statutory basis and found an organisational home within government - probably at Registers of Scotland.

The creation of the first primitive version of the register can be the occasion for the development of some needed standards and definitions:

- an API/machine-readable standard
- a legal definition of a register which can later be incorporated into the Interpretation And Legislative Reform (Scotland) Act (2010).[32]

Working Paper 5.1 *Law reform for data* contains detailed discussions of the critical role of this register in the information architecture going forward.

Introduction to election and politics recommendations

The first set of recommendations about in-service were about rebalancing statistics and audit towards proper representation of non-functional & infrastructural concerns - making things visible.

This set of recommendations are the same thing from the other side - increasing the ability of political parties, think tanks, journalists, 3rd sector bodies and civic society to

32 https://www.legislation.gov.uk/asp/2010/10/contents

consume that information, to turn openness into political pressure.

Recommendation 3 - widening access to data

Description

There is a general right of access to data under Freedom of Information – subject to strict limitations regarding protection for personal data. Social scientists, medical researchers, think tankers and others need access to anonymised data that is stripped of personal information.

Unfortunately modern life is embedded in such an array of data collectors that depersonalised data can often be trivially re-personalised by using data matching techniques to restore the sanitised portions.

Research Data Scotland[33] (RDS) is a Scottish-government funded charitable body that allows accredited researchers access to depersonalised data for research purposes.

This data is provided under an academic user agreement with penalties for misuse and provided solely in safe sandboxed environments.

Each data release agreement is currently bespoke and hand-crafted.

There are a number of issues here:

- is this really an appropriate legal framework for a body that performs a strategic function?
- is the process of releasing data to the RDS under

33 https://www.researchdata.scot/

appropriate constitutional scrutiny?

- is the current legal basis the correct one? should it be required-to-provide instead of able-to-provide?
- how do we make build-to-release-depersonalised into a thing?

There are competing rights that need to be addressed, publicly and systematically:

- the right of individuals to privacy
- the right of society to have access to critical data

But for this to work there need to be obligations on the state too:

- state bodies must release data for examination by the public (or researchers acting in the public interest) via appropriate mechanisms

These competing rights and the obligations necessary to make them maximally successful need to be brought into and designed as a single access regime.

Institutional basis

This will initially be a task for the DSRO and will end up being put on a statutory basis. The citizen's protection part of it needs to be put in a Data Bill of Rights.

Legislation Required 3 - *an Enabling Act*

Legislation Required 8 - *obligation to release data*

Legislation Required 10 - *a Data Bill of Rights*

Development

The DSRO and RDS will need to work out a one-stop mechanism to get data flowing and then implement that.

There might be legal issues that prevent this being

streamlined - and in that case the Enabling Act will need to be used (see Working Paper 8 *An Enabling Act*).

Recommendation 4 - widening access to research fellowships

Description

This project has been conducted under the First Minister's Digital Fellowship Programme. Prior Digital Fellows have been recruited for operational and not research roles.

The proposal is to make Research Fellowships permanently available to develop radical new proposals for the operation of state functions using new technology.

The ability of political parties - and their supporting apparatus of think tanks and civic society to develop more oven-ready policy programmes is a critical part of the health of the political ecosystem.

At the moment policy programmes presented to the electorate are largely aspirational in nature as those proposing them are too far from day-to-day operational reality to make them more concrete.

Digital Fellows work as civil servants and are covered by the civil service social media policy.

The very small Scottish think tank community struggles to fund and execute work. On top of this they are on the outside peering in. This proposal would allow them access and enable them to be more radical and effective.

This research was conducted without the Scottish government paying my wages. Relying on unpaid work is not a sustainable model. If think tanks can't pay wages themselves then additional access is of no use to them. Research fellowships should be government funded.

Scottish Government would be a host organisation providing emails, laptops, heating, lighting and general facilities - but day to day operations would remain with the sponsoring bodies (think tanks, universities etc) and the actual host supervisor inside SG.

This would require a more formal code of conduct for the researchers.

Institutional basis

This is a matter of simple government policy.

Recommendation 5 - Short money considerations

Description

The parliament (and the opposition parties) need to have the tools and expertise to perform effective oversight and engage with the new governmental organisations and the new state capability that this report aims to deliver.

Plurality and healthy debate in the policy ecosystem needs to be supported - and opposition parties in particular need to develop operational depth in their understanding of how the state works, both to be able to provide appropriate scrutiny in Parliament and to be able to best prepare for government.

The Short Money and party support mechanisms at Holyrood should be reviewed to ensure that - to source and fund people with operational and deep technical understanding to work with parliamentarians.

Institutional basis

This is the responsibility of the Scottish Parliament Corporate Body.

Introduction to Government institutions and the programme for government recommendations

This section introduces the core government institution, the Digital Services Reform Office (DSRO) that will provide strategic direction on the various non-functional & infrastructural requirements of a modern integrated digital state, leaving the functional side - ***what*** the state does, as opposed to ***how*** it does it - to the elected Government to drive.

This institution is a pre-legislative body helping to strategically shape the government's programme of work. Its parliamentary oversight body, and in many ways twin, is the Digital Services Scrutiny & Audit Commission. The work of these bodies can only be understood in the context of each other.

The *Programme for Government* is the name of a document laid before Holyrood and is a parliamentary event - and the programme for government in a looser sense is just *what the government is going to do over the next 18 months.*

These recommendations flutter between the formal and informal definitions - they are about increasing the capability of the Scottish state to plan and execute services and systems based on digital systems by whatever means.

Recommendation 6 - create a Digital Services Reform Office

Overview

This recommendation spans many aspects of the full cycle and is split into a number of sub-recommendations. It starts with the institution and then discusses some of its tasks that will be incrementally addressed and its involvement with them:

- changing the PLU's Bill Handbook
- improving organisational support for the PLU and Bill Teams
- making non-functional & infrastructural work visible in the Programme for Government
- a law reform process for data
- developing and proposing Machinery of Government changes
- run the strategic research programme
- participate in a joint review of legislative processes with the parliament
- a user-centred design roadshow
- building an information architecture

The DSRO, its wider role and its integration into parliamentary processes has been extensively discussed earlier - this section is much more task based.

Legislation Required 1 - *putting the DSRO on a statutory basis*

Recommendation 6.1 - the foundations of the DSRO

Description

In many respects the DSRO is the institutionalising of the existing work programme of the Digital Directorate which has been engaged in an extended programme of driving standards, capabilities and componentisation across Scottish Government.

In its final state the DSRO will:

- adopt and publish[34] a charter
- develop and publish its rules of governance and working in public - rhyming with the institutional arrangements of internet governance bodies
- co-work with its counterparts in other jurisdictions
- develop and lay a strategic plan for the non-functional & infrastructural elements of the state before Parliament, including:
  - standards
  - components
    - technical
    - organisational
    - legislative
      - in the Interpretation and Legislative Reform Act
      - in the Parliamentary Counsel's Guidance On Instructing Counsel: Common Legislative Solutions[35]

---

34 A draft charter can be found in Working Paper 10 *Jeff Bezos' API Mandate but for government*

35 https://www.gov.scot/binaries/content/documents/govscot/publicatio

    - infrastructural central services
    - tooling
- propose and supervise the development of components at all levels
- develop and test infrastructural central services, and when they have been encapsulated into an operational organisation facilitate their transition to departmental oversight, in particular:
    - the new proposed statutory registers
        - Legislation Required 4 - *new register of services*
        - Legislation Required 5 - *new register of powers*
        - Legislation Required 6 - *new register of policy*
- manage the development and publication of standards
    - data standards
        - in particular addressing issues raised in Working Paper 1.2 *Data and the rule of law* and wrapping those standards in an appropriate training programme for technical staff to maximise benefits, including filtering and decommissioning
    - technical standards
    - design standards
    - process standards
    - and any other appropriate

---

ns/advice-and-guidance/2018/01/guidance-instructing-counsel-common-legislative-solutions/documents/00530013-pdf/00530013-pdf/govscot%3Adocument/00530013.pdf

- publish guidance on best practice and procedure
- propose legislative changes to both the UK and Scottish governments to enable digitisation - in the Scottish case via Legislation Required 3 - *An Enabling Act*
- develop a law reform process for data (in conjunction with the Scottish Law Reform Commission) which standardises the way in which powers to collect and process data are expressed in legislation and captures those powers in a register. This point is discussed separately as a sub-recommendation in its own right.
- review the use of data across the public sector and recommend data and process consolidation and structural changes (machinery of government (MoG) changes). This point is discussed separately as a sub-recommendation in its own right.
- run the strategic research programme and commission new research. This point is discussed separately as a sub-recommendation in its own right.
- take direction from the government as to directions and proposals to research, develop and bring forward
- plan and supervise work to encapsulate both standards and procedures in open source tooling and provide governance for those projects post development
- develop an appropriate testing practice in the civil service to ensure that systems and services are designed to tested up front and execute the strategic shift from downstream, last-thought, Quality Assurance to top of the stack Quality Engineering
- issue enforcement orders and report malefactors to both the government and its parliamentary overseer

the DSS&AC

It will have a duty to consider the ethical implications of its technical proposals and will be explicitly expected to answer for that to the DSS&AC It will have a ministerial oversight line leading to the Deputy First Minister and the Finance Function.[36]

Some of the work of this new institution is internal to it, but there are three interlocking public elements in this work where it must integrate with other parts of government:

- changing what first the bill teams do, and then all policy development
- helping the bill teams to do it more effectively
- putting in place the declarative part where the Ministers place a political commitment behind the work in the Bill Pack, and a related day-to-day process - this will be discussed in the following recommendations:
  - 8.1 - *changes to the Bill Pack for primary legislation*
  - 8.2 - *changes to the Explanatory Notes for secondary legislation*
  - 8.3 - *approvals process for day-to-day services implementation*

What the DSRO will not do

Given the importance of this institution it is important to outline what it won't do. Departments and agencies will continue to:

- hold budgets

---

36 See the discussion in Recommendation 6.6 - the development and proposition of Machinery of Government changes

- choose implementation technologies
- own delivery dates and programme plans
- do hiring, training and skills management
- do project and programme management
- commission and purchase their own support systems like HR, Finance, Desktop Management, etc, etc
- be responsible to parliament via their minister and their Senior Responsible Officer for the functional and non-functional & infrastructural aspects of their programme

The DSRO is a weak centre and should do as little as possible, *but no less*.

However, the state should perform its core competencies and departments should not be outsourcing software development of main line of business systems to commercial companies.

DETAILED DISCUSSION

The intention is that the DSRO is the strategic technical legal organ of the state. It performs a key co-ordination role across the entire Scottish state, and it its integration with the overarching UK state and external technical communities.

It is designed to be weak, and to operate at a distance via technical standards. The aim is explicitly *co-ordination without communication*, purposeful decoupling of delivery teams in government departments from each other and the centre. A lot of detailed thought has gone into the design of this organisation, its power and precedents, its relationship with the DSS&AC and other state bodies, how it should work and with whom it should work. This thinking includes a full blown theory of state.

More detailed discussion can be found in the relevant working papers:

- Working Paper 0.3 *The locus of change*
- Working Paper 8 *An Enabling Act*
- Working Paper 10.2 *Immediate Hygenic Measures*
- Working Paper 11.1 *Jeff Bezos' Memo, but for government*
- Working Paper 12 *A theory of state*
- Working Paper 13 *A weak centre*

Institutional basis

The DSRO is a government body - it starts as an internal staffing matter and ends on a statutory basis not dissimilar to that created by the Simpler, Faster, Better Services Act[37] in Ontario.

The key officers will be civil servants, supported by an advisory board of technical experts from the private sector.

Those officers will have direct personal responsibility to parliament via the DSS&AC. This will be discussed in more detail in Recommendation 16 - *changes to lines of responsibility in the civil service* and will be in effect the heads of their professions across Scottish Government.

It will be a general staff of the digital state with standing capability in driving strategic data and organisational changes and the definition of core non-functional & infrastructural services.

Legislation Required 1 - *putting the DSRO on a statutory*

37 https://www.ontario.ca/laws/statute/19s07

basis

Development

The iterative development of the two institutions, the DSRO and the DSS&AC, and the finalisation of the parliamentary committee structure that sits over them, will be dealt with in detail in the implementation section.

Recommendation 6.2 - changes to the PLU's Bill Handbook

Description

All the jurisdictions in the UK publish handbooks for Bill Teams that describe the process of creating a bill and taking it through parliament. The Scottish version is the *Bill Handbook.*[38]

The handbooks either don't mention digital systems, data or service and operational design or mention it only in passing.

The evidence from technical teams is *they should have spoken to us earlier.*

One of the overarching aims of this reform process is to close the gap between policy, delivery and in-service teams. Integrated team work is best practice across the UK civil service, but it is not yet habitual and usual practice – its has not become the air we breathe.

---

[38] https://www.gov.scot/binaries/content/documents/govscot/publications/foi-eir-release/2022/07/foi-202200306018/documents/foi-202200306018---information-released/foi-202200306018---information-released/govscot:document/FOI%2B202200306018%2B-%2BInformation%2Breleased.pdf

The handbook should include sections about considering:

- what data is going to be used
- who has, or can provide that data
- what existing infrastructure should be reused, for example:
    - sign-ons
    - payment rails
    - address look-ups
- who the delivery team are
- what impact there will be on existing services
- how success and failure will be measured
- what metrics will be developed

The existing Digital Directorate will need to help the PLU make the appropriate changes to the *Bill Handbook* as part of its transition to the DSRO.

The goal is to drive behavioural changes and have the critical design and reuse discussions earlier in the process.

INSTITUTIONAL BASIS

The PLU owns the handbook - the Digital Directorate has the expertise to change it.

Some changes will be implemented in Legislation Required 7 - *amendments to The Interpretation And Legislative Reform (Scotland) Act 2011*

DEVELOPMENT

Changes to the PLU *Bill Handbook* will be ongoing and iterative. It starts with the simple hygienic measures listed here. Some of those questions will be turned into products, services, amendments of the Interpretation and Legislative

Reform (Scotland) Act 2010[39] and patterns in the Parliamentary Counsel's *Guidance On Instruction Counsel: Common Legislative Solutions.*[40]

As componentisation and infrastructure service creation develops question likes *you should think about how you will send or receive money* will become statements like *you will be using the Scottish payment rails and details of how it works can be found here, here and here.* This is discussed in Working Paper 3 *The Lego state.*

Recommendation 6.3 - improved organisational support for the PLU and Bill Teams

Description

This recommendation backs off the changes to the PLU *Bill Handbook.* There is structural support for Bill Teams in developing their Financial Memorandum for the bill pack, this is the equivalent for the proposed Systems Impact Assessment.

As civil servants flow through the bill process they will inevitably come from departments with different levels of digital capabilities. Some will be from expert joint policy-delivery teams. But some will suffer from policy-isolation, or lack access to technical, design, data or delivery skills. This team is the tip of the spear for addressing those issues before

---

39 https://www.legislation.gov.uk/asp/2010/10/contents

40 https://www.gov.scot/binaries/content/documents/govscot/publications/advice-and-guidance/2018/01/guidance-instructing-counsel-common-legislative-solutions/documents/00530013-pdf/00530013-pdf/govscot%3Adocument/00530013.pdf

teams get too deep in the legislative process. But is also a scout for training and upskilling activities to help the day to day work of the same departments.

Institutional basis

This is a Scottish Government staffing and organisational issue.

Development

The team who do this will be the seed-germ of the DSRO that will grow into the full institution.

The PLU is itself a central support unit reporting to the Minister for Parliament - the Bill Teams however are drawn from many directorates and report to many ministers.

Engaging with Bill Teams on helping them prepare for the Systems Impact Assessment is therefore a key opportunity for the digital specialists to assess which sections of the Scottish Government need what additional help or training and develop programmes to do that. It is a senior job - even if the formal description could be done by more junior staff.

This team therefore is working incrementally towards a strategic position, with strategic powers and needs to acquire strategic understanding by doing the job.

Recommendation 6.4 - make non-functional & infrastructural work visible in the Programme for Government

DESCRIPTION

The *Programme for Government* is a work in progress report that is presented to the Scottish Parliament each September. It presents the work the government is undertaking over the next 12 months and beyond into the medium term.

The major institutional and non-functional & infrastructural activities are scarcely visible in it - see Working Paper 9.1 *Reading legislation with a non-functional eye*.

As part of rebalancing the state away from a structural focus on functional requirements this needs to change.

INSTITUTIONAL BASIS

Programme for Government is under the control of the Scottish Government.

Recommendation 6.5 - a law reform process for data

DESCRIPTION

This activity has been pulled out as a sub-recommendation on its own as account of its size and importance. It is discussed in great detail in Working Paper 5.1 Law *Reform for data*.

Fundamental clarity about what powers exist for the

collection of data, what data is being held by which government department and with whom can it and it is being shared is a strategic capability which will shape society and politics for the next hundred years.

The clarification of the legislation needs to be driven from an operational perspective.

Implementation of the law reform will be a gradual and incremental process. The benefits of it must be reaped incrementally. Working Paper 6 *A solera for data cleansing* lays out a possible mechanism for the phasing of that work. The goal is to get state data cleaned up and available to the widest possible audiences in a machine readable format as soon as possible. We cannot afford to wait for a 10 year programme to complete.

Institutional basis

This recommendation touches the government, which drafts legislation, the parliament, which approves it, and the judiciary and legal profession, who care strongly about the format and structure of it. It is a delicate constitutional issue. The Scottish Law Commission should bring its expertise to bear on it.

The legislation required is:

Legislation Required 3 - *an Enabling Act*

Legislation Required 4 - *new register of services*

Legislation Required 5 - *new register of powers*

Recommendation 6.6 - the development and proposition of Machinery of Government changes

Description

Traditionally Machinery of Government (MoG) changes are the prerogative of the First Minister/Prime Minister. This proposal therefore represents a significant change - and has been pulled out for more discussion.

It also highlights why the Ministerial line over DSRO should be the DFM/Finance Function.

MoG (rightly) has a bad reputation – oftentimes its *something must be done, here I am doing something.*

There is a strategic operational approach to MoG changes that derives from data management. If two data sources can be consolidated, then the processes that operate on that data can be consolidated, and if the processes are consolidated then the organisations that execute them can be.

This process is the subject of extensive discussion in Working Paper 3 *The Lego state,* Working Paper 5.1 *Law Reform for data* and Working Paper 6 *A solera for data cleansing.*

The state needs to have the strategic capability to assess the data landscape, cross-match that with operational and financial data and identify opportunities for process and organisational consolidation.

It is this strategic function that implies that the DSRO should sit with the DFM/Finance as a cross-departmental, co-ordinating activity.

The structural transformation that the internet has

wreaked across many service businesses in the private sector is driven by this process.

The anecdote *why do I have to go through this again with you when I have already told you this* is the mark of an opportunity for consolidation.

Consolidation reduces the cost of providing state services, frees money to be spent better elsewhere by the state or citizen, and reduces the amount of time the citizen has to spend engaging with state organs.

Experience also shows that the process of looking for data consolidation opportunities also highlights orphan and redundant data collection processes that can be stopped.

Institutional basis

This is a convention.

Development

This recommendation depends on the standards and data reporting process reaching a fairly advanced state of maturity and will be consequent on Recommendation 6.5 *a law reform for data* being completed. Technical capability such as that outlined by Working Paper 6 *A solera for data cleansing* will need to be in place.

Recommendation 6.7 - *run the strategic research programme and commission new research*

Recommendation 6.7 - run the strategic research programme and commission new research

Description

A proposed set of research activities to be executed by CivTech under the supervision of the DSRO were outlined earlier in the report as a pump primer (Further details are in Appendix 5 *CivTech Research Proposals*).

They are:

- the 4 rules as code projects:
    - generating MVPs as part of policy and legislative design
    - macro-economic modelling
    - property-based testing
    - reducing barriers to legislative compliance
- components
- remixability
- revisiting on-prem and global scale capacity

The DSRO should progress with them as it sees fit and develop and propose other research projects based on the development of the standards- and components-driven state.

The outputs of these research proposals should feed into 6.9 *a user-centred design roadshow.*

Institutional basis

This is day to day operations of the Scottish state.

Recommendation 6.8 - participation in a joint review of legislative processes with the parliament

Description

This process will be parliament-led and is described in more detail in Recommendation 11 - *a review of legislative processes for major digital programmes.*

The DSRO will have to design the process, brief the minister and support them in negotiation with the parliament to get their participation and manage the handover to the joint team who will do the actual work.

Institutional basis

This will be quasi-constitutional joint working of the government and the parliament.

Recommendation 6.9 - a user-centred design roadshow

Description

The transformative effect of exposing politicians to user-centred design was a common theme from interviewees that crossed departments (Home Office, Ministry of Justice, DWP, Social Security Scotland, Digital Directorate) and jurisdictions (Westminster, Scotland, Ontario).

Politicians are now quite familiar with user-centred research in the context of political focus groups and understand both the power and pitfalls of the approach.

Many of the recommendations in this report put user-centred design and the creation of shared artefacts (MVPs, paper-prototypes, etc) front and centre. They are simply the best techniques to drive consensus across different professions by making the abstract concrete.

Whilst the work of developing the new processes is being done, it should be actively promoted to both Ministers and Parliamentarians as well as civil servants. This proposal should be regarded as a mechanism for building culture change across the piece. Everyone is equal in front of a tangible prototype.

Over time the contents of this roadshow should come from 6.7 *run the strategic research programme and commission new research.*

Institutional basis

This is day to day work of government.

Recommendation 6.10 - an information architecture

Description

On a couple of occasions during this research it became clear that are genuine problems with the current way in which Scottish government documents are published. Whilst examining the issues discussed in Appendix 4 *Failure to manage non-functionals/infrastructurals in the public sector* it became clear that some recent documents are simply no longer on government websites. The production process of this report was another unexpected one.

One of the most consequential economic changes of the

21st century, the shift of Amazon from a bookseller to a global provider of computing power, suffers from the same problem. Key decisions have to be reconstructed from memory because the documentation has gone into a digital black hole.

Government needs to have a clear information architecture that allows policies, reviews, standards and publications to be announced, superseded, and retired, all the while being able to be found and studied. *What's on the website is current, what isn't isn't* is not an information architecture. A restrictive outsourced contract is no way to run a core government function.

The digital state requires librarianship, document design and communication excellence to be baked into its design and technical capability.

The DSRO will not be able to operate as an externally engaged, cross-jurisdictional organisation that consults widely on complex technical standards under the current publication restrictions.

Institutional basis

This is day to day work of government.

Recommendation 7 - review the process of creating legislation for local government and other sub-state bodies

Description

Unfortunately pressure of time prevented me from exploring the issue of the relationship of the central state to the partitioned sub-state in enough detail - in particular I was unable to talk to enough practitioners in local government to come to any useful conclusions.

This recommendation is that someone else is commissioned to do that review - building on this one - and explore the relationship between a legislative layer of the state and its subordinates.

This relation is bi-directional in the UK, with Scotland having Westminster over it and local government below it. Westminster is subordinate to the EU in relation to its relations with Stormont.

The European Union - as an institution with a weak centre that has little operational capability - has wrestled with this issue for a number of years. Understanding and conceptualising the EU structure of law making, with its separation of objectives and implementation in the process is key to this.

When central organs legislate for sub-ordinate ones they should do in the context of functional autonomy - describing what objectives the law should have and not the means that the sub-ordinate body chooses to achieve them. The question of whether the implementation matches the objectives then becomes justiciable.

The goal is to make delivery teams as autonomous as possible, and that doesn't stop at autonomy over implementation, its needs as much autonomy over finance, scheduling, hiring and resourcing as possible.

The European Union is also starting to implement legislation defining data interchange between autonomous subordinates - for things like taxation. This is an area of great interest at a sub-state level.

This model would be part of any transformed legislative structure and process for partitioned sub-state bodies - variety in implementation, uniformity in intercommunication.

In particular the research should look at possible new legislative paths for legislation proposing partitioned data across sub-state bodies, with changed consultation and approval models.

INSTITUTIONAL BASIS

This can be commissioned by the Scottish Government directly.

Introduction - the Bill Pack, etc recommendations

This section has the ambiguous title to include new elements that don't exist in the current development cycle - to wit digital standards.

There are three routes from the programme for government to delivery - primary and secondary legislation goes through parliament, day to day activities do not.

The computer doesn't care. From the purpose of improving processes we need to ensure that the same gross oversight and design standards are enforced however the project progresses.

For the parliamentary routes, one of the key proposals in this report is the transfer of detailed design from post-legislation to pre-.

The introduction of legislation into parliament is a liminal point. And here we can apply a simple technique that is pervasive in high-quality organisational contexts (surgery, plane and space flight, etc): the humble checklist.

In the crudest sense the Bill Pack is the proposed legislation and a set of checklists that show the introducing Minister has considered all the identified issues and that the process of bill drafting is of high quality.

We have seen previously that the text of the bill itself contains functional specifications only, but that there are no non-functional & infrastructural specifications - and yet there will be no digital systems without the latter.

This is the point at which the relevant non-functional & infrastructural requirements (whether standards, or systems that need to be integrated) are attached to the functional specification in the law to create a more complete and unitary point of specification.

The two things in this section are a new Systems Impact Assessment in the Bill Pack and the formal publication of standards which that SIA references and which are formal constraints and obligations on the delivery of software and systems functionally defined by the text of the Bill.

For the day to day route these same checks need to be implemented - in this case by an internal government process and not a parliamentary process.

Recommendation 8 - changes to the Bill Pack, etc

There are three different flows of specifications for digital systems from conception to delivery. They go via primary legislation, secondary legislation and day to day work.

The balance and division of labour between primary and secondary legislation is a subject of interest - and

Recommendation 11 - *a review of legislative processes for major digital programmes* will interrogate that in part.

The bill pack is a critical hinge point - where the functional requirements of the legislation are to be married to the non-functional & infrastructural requirements for an integrated specification.

There are three sub-recommendations - one each for the primary and secondary and day-to-day routes.

Recommendation 8.1 - changes to the Bill Pack for primary legislation

Description

A civil service mantra to live by is *don't embarrass your minister*. Of all the opportunities to do so, the introduction of a new bill is probably the most high profile.

The new Service Impact Assessment will be part of the Bill Pack. It contains a range of new elements covering:

- what process has been followed:
    - if appropriate including or referencing artefacts produced in the process that enable better understanding, for example:
        - paper prototypes
        - MVPs
        - business architectures
- if success metrics, using both operational data and statistical surveys, have been developed
- details of data use/reuse/publication, etc
- what the success criteria for the policy are

    - how they relate with the National Performance Framework
    - what the review cycle for evaluating success will be
- formal statements of non-functional & infrastructural requirements
    - mandated use of particular non-functional & infrastructural services
        - for example payments or identity
    - external systems to which integration is prioritised
        - for example joined up geographical data
- standards being complied with

This in turn makes the Bill Pack a critical change management tool to drive new ways of working. If the Minister says *we followed the new processes and did all the things we promised to do* in the chamber then the team better have done so. When the Minister declares *this is how it will be delivered* then the delivery team better deliver.

This effectively promotes a number of issues raised in the Bill Pack training from *nice to have done* to *this is the air we breathe* normality.

And as the Bill Pack is formally a child of the Parliament and not the Government, the introduction of new elements into it plays a critical role in *Explicite* - the process of making the digital development cycle explicit and part of a shared understanding - and not *that's what they do, nothing to do with me.*

INSTITUTIONAL BASIS

The format of the Bill Pack is formally under the control of the Scottish Parliament Corporate Body who determine its proper form.

Development

There will be a number of iterative changes to the proper form as the institutions mature.

Recommendation 8.2 - changes to the Explanatory Notes for secondary legislation

Description

There are two changes required for appropriate pieces of secondary legislation.

Where the regulations contained in secondary legislation are expected to be turned into digital systems the Explanatory Notes should state the expected release date of the software update that will implement the update and if that date is after the Commencement Date it will describe any manual workarounds that will be put in place in the interim. The responsibility for setting the software release date will be on delivery managers.[41]

Normally secondary legislation alters the operation of an extant system in some way, sometimes simply changing static data (the value of an inflation rate specified in a table) and sometimes in substantial ways.

To help parliamentarians (and Ministers) better understand the impact of secondary legislation rule-of-thumb

---

[41] This is covered by Recommendation 15 - changes to lines of responsibility in the civil service

impact assessments based on Business Architectures (which mature government departments will have already) should be included. These take the form *this is a 3 sub-system change, that is a 9 sub-system change*. This will have the effect of driving the use of rule-of-thumb assessments in the development of policy across the board and provides a cheap and cheerful mechanism for this-or-that decisions..

This rule-of-thumb approach is already in use in some parts of the civil service and should be generalised.

Institutional basis

The format of the Explanatory Notes for secondary legislation is formally under the control of the Scottish Parliament Corporate Body who determine its proper form.

Development

After the work on designing new digital legislative processes there may well be additional changes to the format and structure of the pack associated with secondary legislation.

Recommendation 8.3 - approvals process for day-to-day services implementation

Description

There are services being deployed on a day-to-day basis that do not touch parliament. The Bill Pack and Explanatory Notes are being used to impose a checklist on service working going down those routes.

The same checklist needs to be applied to the day-to-day

process but by different mechanisms. There are existing large project review processes for Scottish Government and in Westminster, and the Ontario Digital Services implemented a similar one.

Institutional basis

This is under the control of Scottish Government.

Development

This is really an alignment process - the 3 sub-recommendations under Recommendation 8 are close cousins and need to be thought about and implemented together.

Recommendation 9 - a new gazette to publish technical standards in

Description

The introduction of legislation is an important event in the life of the state. Legislation includes functional requirements, the bill pack and standards cover the non-functionals/infrastructurals. The unification of functional and non-functional & infrastructural specifications is a key goal - *this is* **what** *will be done, and this is* **how** *it will be done* - unity of specification. This recommendation is the mechanism by which the non-functional & infrastructural specifications are published.

The bill pack will be making statements about compliance - and the standards, guidelines and use of mandatory infrastructure to which things will be expected to comply are correspondingly an important part of the story.

The parliament will have a new institution under its control to help it understand the consequences and whether the proposals will, in the round, achieve their objectives.

The standards then are part of the formal process of decisioning and need to be treated with the appropriate level of dignity. They need to be openly published, formally amended with the ability to determine which standards were in force at some past point in time. In short they resemble laws and need to be published as registers so they can be enumerated and interrogated both synchronously and diachronically.

The standards and guidelines aren't law, but do rhyme with it. Correspondingly the new gazette isn't legislation.gov.uk but rhymes with it.

Institutional basis

The legislation required is:

Legislation Required 1 - *putting the DSRO on a statutory basis*

Legislation Required 7 - *amendments to The Interpretation And Legislative Reform (Scotland) Act 2011*

Development

In the initial days these standards will be maintained informally and published via git.[42] before being formalised.

---

[42] git is a version control programme used across the internet sector

Introduction to Parliamentary institutions and processes

The recommendations in this area cover a range of different things - new institutions, changes to an existing one, changes to standing orders, changes to how the parliament exposes itself to public and academic scrutiny.

Some of these recommendations are minor and consequential to recommendations elsewhere in the development cycle - for instance a change to the Bill Pack implies a change to Standing Orders.

The new parliamentary institution, the Digital Services Scrutiny & Audit Commission (DSS&AC) is the central recommendation though - the oversight body of the corresponding government body the Digital Services Reform Office (DSRO). These twin institutions can only be understood in the context of each other.

A number of other recommendations will involve changes to the Standing Orders:

- 7 - *review the process of creating legislation for local government and other sub-state bodies*
- 8.1 - *changes to the Bill Pack for primary legislation*
- 8.2 - *changes to the Explanatory Notes for secondary legislation*

Recommendation 10 - create a Digital Services Scrutiny & Audit Commission

Description

The DSS&AC is the supervisory body of the DSRO. It will sit under a parliamentary committee in the same way the Scottish Commission on Social Security sits under the Social Justice and Social Security Committee.

At this stage it is not clear what that committee would be - the final committee arrangements will become clear as the implementation plan progresses. Options are canvassed in Working Paper 0.3 *The locus of change*.

The DSS&AC has two core functions as its name suggests, it will act as:

- an audit body
  - compliance with standards
  - implementation of best practices
  - correct major project initiation and start up
  - commission and execution of surface audits:
    - usability
    - compliance with accessibility
  - the public operations of the DSRO and its relationship with both the internal technical communities and external jurisdictions
- a scrutiny body
  - supporting its parent parliamentary committee, and any other appropriate functional/bill committee in scrutinising appropriate aspects of

primary legislation
- acting as a triage and filter point for secondary legislation for both its parent committee and the Delegated Powers & Law Reform Committee
- reviewing standards and guidance that have been issued by the DSRO under its own recognisance

As an audit body it will have the power to compel. Key officials of the DSRO and individuals in major digital programmes will have a personal line of accountability to it. This is discussed in Recommendation 16 - *changes to lines of responsibility in the civil service.*

The DSS&AC is not a purely technical body - it must consider technical infrastructure in the round and in addition to technical specialists its members will include:

- social scientists
- ethicists
- legal experts

This body has similarities to the Scottish Commission for Social Security which is a triage and filter point for Social Security secondary legislation. However that body oversees functional matters of social security - this body is entirely concerned with non-functional & infrastructural matters.

The relationship of parliament to the supervision of functional requirements will be addressed in more detail in Recommendation 11 *a review of legislative processes for major digital programme.*

This body works alongside the Audit Commission and there is a legitimate debate to had about the hard audit functions like the execution of usability and accessibility audits.

These hard audits are a powerful tool because of the hygienic nature of the tests. In order for a system to have good usability and accessibility written onto their surface affect, a whole host of earlier and harder to measure stages must be of high quality, including:

- design
- programme management and resource allocation
- testing and assurance

It might be more appropriate to get Audit Scotland to extend their remit and capabilities slightly and have these audits done by them using the existing charge back mechanisms in place for financial audit.

Institutional basis

This will be a statutory body and it will sit under a parliamentary committee. Its introduction will involve an adjustment and rearrangement of committees of the Scottish Parliament and a consequential set of adjustments in Standing Orders.

Legislation Required 2 - *putting the DSS&AC on a statutory basis*

Development

The iterative development of the two institutions, the DSRO and the DSS&AC, and the finalisation of the parliamentary committee structure that sits over them, will be dealt with in detail in the implementation section.

Recommendation 11 - a review of legislative processes for major digital programmes

Description

This recommendation is described in great detail in Working Paper 7.3 *Experimental digital legislative processes.*

The recommendation flows from two incontrovertible facts:

- that laws are not point-in-time events with regard to iterative development of major digital systems
- the process of writing the law is mutable and can be adapted to lead to better and more effective design and oversight of digital systems

A number of possible options have been developed and this recommendation is that there is a formal review processes based on a paper exercise refighting the Scottish Social Security wars on a table and make recommendations as to changes to parliamentary process.

The proposal will be worked up by the DSRO and the subject of negotiation between the government and the parliament, but the work should be parliament-led.

Institutional basis

This review will propose changes to the format of legislation and the underlying Standing Orders.

It may require changes to Section 36[43] of the Scotland Act 1998.

---

43 https://www.legislation.gov.uk/ukpga/1998/46/section/36

Recommendation 12 - publication of legislative amendments

Description

A common drafting and legislation management tool is used by parliamentary counsel in drafting bills, by clerks taking bills and amendments through the parliamentary process, and managing post-assent amendment to extant legislation.

The initial drafting process is private, the bill emerges when it is lodged with the parliamentary clerks and is published on the Scottish Parliament website.

Its amended forms after each stage are also published.

After assent it is published on legislation.gov.uk[44] and as changes are made to it the published version is amended (with a version history).

The various amendments tabled and not selected for debate, or debated and rejected are noted on the parliamentary website but not released in the machine readable format that underlies the tools and that are used to manage amendment of the final legislation.

The recommendation is that the facility to publish them as XML is turned on and the internal decision making process of the parliament is made more open and amenable to academic study.

Institutional basis

This is under the control of the Scottish Parliament Corporate Body.

---

44 http://legislation.gov.uk

Recommendation 13 - additional capabilities for SPICe

Description

The Scottish Parliament Information Centre (SPICe) currently don't have specialist support for digital issues. When the DSS&AC is created with its own specialist members, then SPICe needs to adjust to support parliamentarians alongside it.

Institutional basis

This is a day to day management issue for SPICe and the Scottish Parliamentary Corporate Body.

Introduction to testing recommendations

By and large this report makes few recommendations regarding technical trades - largely confining itself to changing where in the process cycle activities take place.

One of the reasons for this is the general absence of evidence for missing technical skills, techniques or infrastructure - testing being the exception that proves the rule.

Testing is a bit of a cinderella in the public services with no established quality community.

There is a research project which might enable dramatic cost savings using Property-Based Testing - this also makes testing something of a special case. See Appendix 5 - *CivTech Research Proposals*. This sub-proposal is also the only substantially functional recommendation in the report - the rest being non-functional & infrastructural.

Recommendation 14 - testing needs to be made a first class professional discipline in Government

Description

There is currently no formal community of practice for testing, quality assurance or quality engineering in the GB civil service. Testing is considered just an activity done at the end of software development.

A mature organisation would have a Quality Engineering function that designs systems to be tested for functional correctness and adherence to the rule of law and is engaged at the early design stage (as part of the pre-legislative processes).

One of the research projects formally explores property-based testing integrated with legislative drafting that should be the occasion of developing that capability.

Institutional basis

This a government and organisation HR issue.

Introduction to delivery recommendations

One of the key thrusts of this report is the devolution of autonomy to delivery and departmental teams. In addition the rebalancing of functional and non-functional & infrastructural specification across the state gives these teams two masters - their traditional departmental chiefs for the functional side and the new institutions in this report for the other. This recommendation deals with the issues arising from this new world.

Recommendation 15 - changes to lines of responsibility in the civil service

Description

Francis Maude changed both the Ministerial Code[45] and the Osmotherly Rules[46] in response to early failures in Universal Credit.

Specifically responsibility for setting Go Live! dates was moved from Ministers and given to Senior Responsible Officers.[47] A mysterious and unachievable political date had emerged. Nobody from the minister down has been able to trace how that happened. The government found itself on an embarrassing expectations hook.

These changes were not reflected in Scottish Government practice - and they should be, except expanded and deepened.

In Scotland the Commencement Date is formally set by the Minister - usually on advice. But sometimes the Commencement Date is 3 or 6 months before the software release slot with the functionality in it.

---

45 https://assets.publishing.service.gov.uk/media/63a4628bd3bf7f37654767f2/Ministerial_Code.pdf

46 The Osmotherly Rules are a convention that governs how civil servants respond to parliamentary questioning when summoned to give evidence at Westminster

47 Section 5.6 https://assets.publishing.service.gov.uk/media/63a4628bd3bf7f37654767f2/Ministerial_Code.pdf

This creates long running manual workarounds with the attendant extra cost and risk of error and injustice.

This issue is partly addressed in Recommendation 8.2 - *changes to the Explanatory Notes for secondary legislation*. Generally delivery leads should have formal responsibility to parliament for setting Go Live! dates for major systems or software delivery dates for secondary legislation that implements functional changes in systems.

The creation of the DSRO will put the heads of technical professions on a statutory basis with a personal responsibility to the DSS&AC.

The rebalancing of institutions to make non-functionals/infrastructurals more actionable changes the responsibility of individual civil servants.

It is considered normal that some servants of the state have two masters: lawyers have a duty-to-the-courts alongside their chain-of-command responsibility, similarly accountants and doctors have responsibility to their professions.

The creation of the DSRO and the DSS&AC to provide non-functional & infrastructural guidance alongside functional law give members of the technical trades two masters.[48]

Senior Responsible Officers and Senior Accounting Officers already have two masters. They have departmental responsibility to their minister and personal responsibility to parliament with respect to financial aspects[49] of their work.

---

48 See the discussion in Working Paper 13 *The weak centre*

49 See for instance Annex 1 of the Scottish Public Finance Manual. https://www.gov.scot/publications/scottish-public-finance-manual/accountability/annex-1-memorandum-to-accountable-officers-

Section 4.1 of the Osmotherly Rules is forthright in their interpretation of the Civil Service Code:

> *The Civil Service Code makes clear that civil servants are accountable to Ministers who in turn are accountable to Parliament. It therefore follows that when civil servants give evidence to a Select Committee they are doing so, not in a personal capacity, but as representatives of their Ministers.*

The Scottish Ministerial Code,[50] the Scottish Civil Service Code[51] and the Osmotherly Rules need to be updated to accommodate these new two master roles.

The technical leads (GTO, GDaO and GDeO) are directly responsible to Parliament. But they are not Ministers and do not speak on behalf of everyone in their profession. More junior technical staff in departmental and delivery teams need to be directly responsible to the DSS&AC for technical issues.

This mirrors the right of audience for all technical staff at the DSRO.

INSTITUTIONAL BASIS

The two codes are created by the Scottish Government and laid before Parliament.

The Osmotherly Rules are a convention.

---

scottish-administration/ as referenced in Section 6.8 of the Scottish Ministerial Code https://www.gov.scot/publications/scottish-ministerial-code-2023-edition/pages/7/

50 https://www.gov.scot/publications/scottish-ministerial-code-2023-edition/pages/7/

51 https://www.gov.scot/publications/civil-service-code/

CHAPTER ELEVEN
Legislative enactments

Introduction to required legislation

There are a number of different enactments that will be required over the medium term, 3 to 5 years. How they are grouped into Bills will depend on the evolution of the implementation plan. The enactments are:

- *putting the DSRO on a statutory basis*
- *putting the DSS&AC on a statutory basis*
- *an Enabling Act*
- *new register of services*
- *new register of powers*
- *new register of policy*
- *amendments to The Interpretation And Legislative Reform (Scotland) Act 2011*
- *obligation to release data*
- *obligation to publish non-functional & infrastructural statistics*
- *a Data Bill of Rights*

Legislation Required 1 - putting the DSRO on a statutory basis

The new governmental institution, the Digital Systems Reform Office will need to be put on a statutory basis.

The structure of this institution is discussed in more detail in Working Paper 0.3 *The locus of change*. A chunk of its structural form should be taken from the Law Commission Act 1965[52] and the new elements that put standards on a legislative basis from the Ontario Simpler, Faster, Better

52 https://www.legislation.gov.uk/ukpga/1965/22/section/2

Services Act.[53]

This legislation is required by Recommendation 6 - *create a Digital Services Reform Office*

Legislation Required 2 - putting the DSS&AC on a statutory basis

The new parliamentary body the Digital Services Scrutiny & Audit Commission will need to be put on a statutory basis.

The structure of this institution is discussed in more detail in Working Paper 0.3 *The locus of change*. The statute will draw on both the Public Finance And Accounting (Scotland) Act 2000[54] and the Social Security (Scotland) Act 2018.[55]

This legislation is required by Recommendation 10 - *create a Digital Services Scrutiny & Audit Commission.*

Legislation Required 3 - an Enabling Act

There are hard limits to the throughput of parliament – approximately 20-25 Bills per calendar year, and 400-450 Ministerial Orders.

Any proposal to change how the state creates digital systems is Janus-faced, one face looks back to perform law reform on statutes that accidentally impede the best digital practices – and the other face looks forward to change how we specify new systems.

---

53 https://www.ontario.ca/laws/statute/19s07

54 https://www.legislation.gov.uk/asp/2000/1/part/2/enacted

55 https://www.legislation.gov.uk/asp/2018/9/section/22/enacted

The first of these views threatens to overwhelm parliament with primary legislative changes which are intended to alter policy effect but not policy intent.

The experience of the Ontario Digital Service was that 100 Acts needed amendment in their transformation process.

The expected transformation in Scotland will be higher than this, because of the proposal to undertake a full-blown law reform process for data.

Data law reform is discussed extensively in Working Paper 5.1 *Law reform for data.*

The review work for the reform of legislation covering local government and other partitioned sub-state is likely to generate additional legislation as well although it will not be clear that would come directly under this act until the work of the review is completed.

The proposal for an Enabling Act is discussed more extensively in Working Paper 8 *An Enabling A*ct.

This legislation is required by:

- Recommendation 6.1 - *the foundations of the DSRO*
- Recommendation 6.5 - *a law reform process for data*

Legislation Required 4 - new register of services

As part of the legal information architecture outlined in Working Paper 5.1 Law *reform for data* a new statutory register of services will need to be created.

In the interim phases it will just be a simple web site - but it will become statutory.

This legislation is required by:

- Recommendation 2 - *Registers of Services, Powers and Policies*
- Recommendation 6.1 - *the foundations of the DSRO*
- Recommendation 6.5 - *a law reform process for data*

This legislation in its turn depends on the new statutory definition of a register via Legislation Required 7 - *amendments to The Interpretation And Legislative Reform (Scotland) Act 2011*

Legislation Required 5 - new register of powers

As part of the information architecture outlined in Working Paper 5.1 *Law reform for data* a new statutory register of powers will need to be created.

In the interim phases it will just be a simple web site - but it will become statutory.

This legislation is required by:

- Recommendation 6.1 - *the foundations of the DSRO*
- Recommendation 6.5 - *a law reform process for data*

This legislation in its turn depends on the new statutory definition of a register via Legislation Required 7 - *amendments to The Interpretation And Legislative Reform (Scotland) Act 2011*

Legislation Required 6 - new register of policy

There is no formal mechanism that tells citizens and civic society what current policies the government is implementing, when new policies are adopted and when old policies are retired.

There should be a lightweight register of policy which civil servants are required to maintain that lists policies in development, in force, and in retirement.

It should link out to relevant department websites containing details. It needs to be backed off with an enforced information architecture and appropriate tooling that makes document publication on the internet permanent and findable and not transitory as it currently is.

The citizen would be able to enumerate all current policy at a given point in time and then get access to the relevant documents, publications and systems for a given current or past policy.

This legislation is required by

- Recommendation 6.1 - *the foundations of the DSRO*
- Recommendation 2 - *Registers of Services, Powers and Policies*

This legislation in its turn depends on the new statutory definition of a register via Legislation Required 7 - *amendments to The Interpretation And Legislative Reform (Scotland) Act 2011*

Legislation Required 7 - amendments to The Interpretation And Legislative Reform (Scotland) Act 2010

The Interpretation And Legislative Reform (Scotland) Act 2010[56] is a target for the law reform for data process and the componentisation process.

Core data patterns (Registers, Ledgers) will be defined in the Interpretation And Legislative Reform Act – as well as other technical terms that connect the parliament of laws with the parliament of standards by putting technical elements of state computer systems under the rules of gazetted standards.

These amendments will structure the information architecture of the state.

This process is discussed in Working Paper 3 *The Lego state* and Working Paper 5.1 *Law reform for data.*

This legislation is required by:

Recommendation 2 - *Registers of Services, Powers and Policies*

Recommendation 6.2 - *changes to the PLU's Bill Handbook*

It is in turn required by:

Legislation Required 4 - *new register of services*

Legislation Required 5 - *new register of powers*

Legislation Required 6 - *new register of policy*

---

56 https://www.legislation.gov.uk/asp/2010/10/contents

Legislation Required 8 - obligation to publish data

The sharing of anonymised personal data for research purposes via the Research Data Scotland approach should be made a statutory duty.

This would eliminate the continued and bespoke data sharing agreement dance that is currently required to get access to significant state-held databases.

This legislation is required by Recommendation 3 - *widening access to data*

Legislation Required 9 - obligation to publish non-functional & infrastructural statistics

The government will be obliged to collate and publish statistics about the non-functional & infrastructural elements of the state.

The DSS&AC will have an oversight role in developing the format and contents of the statistics.

These statistics will both be operational non-functional measures and external and independent social surveys.

This legislation is required by Recommendation 1 - *an obligation to publish non-functional & infrastructural statistics about state operations*

Legislation Required 10 - a Data Bill of Rights

There is a fundamental tension at the heart of the proposal for digital law reform outlined in Working Paper 5.1 *Law reform for data* and the work of the DSRO as a standards body.

That Working Paper lays out a process for separating out the ***will*** to share data from the ***means*** of sharing data.

That would make it possible to understand and reason about what data is held and available for sharing and what data flows across the public sector in a way that cannot currently be done.

The standards process aims to drive the cost of the ***means*** of sharing data to zero - making any piece of state data technically consumable by any other state service.

Left to itself, lower technical barriers to sharing, higher understanding of what data exists and where it might be useful, and productionised mechanisms for establishing the legal criteria for sharing data will drive up data sharing and reuse.

The state will have set itself up to use *your* data for *its* convenience.

With the rise of social horrors like the Chinese surveillance state this does not seem good.

I am stepping out of the apolitical comfort zone and suggesting a Data Bill of Rights will be required that will put proportionality and privacy at the centre of the data world and put a muzzle on administrative convenience, giving citizens judicial remedy if they think the state has overstepped the bounds.

CHAPTER TWELVE

Implementation Plan

Implementation overview

The work that needs to be done falls into 2 categories:

- complex, multi-body changes
- simple, uncoupled changes

The complex multi-body changes are:

- the creation of new institutions which involves changes to legislation, standing orders, government organisations and parliamentary committees
- the iteration final state

The simple, uncoupled changes are:

- simple steps to improve iteration
- hygienic measures
- research programmes

The fundamental implementation here is the creation of the new institutional structures that are then able to address the complex issue of iteration.

The new structures should be built slowly from a gentle start and the simplest working version and tested, improved and expanded via use.

The first step is the boot strapping of the nascent DSRO - it needs to become the institution it needs to be, before it can start its mission.

The simpler elements, basic iteration and research programmes should be undertaken at leisure.

Co-implementation

This report proposes changes on a 100 year scale to how the state operates - and its recommendations cut across constitutional red lines between the civil service and politics, between government and parliament. It includes proposing changes to:

- the format of legislation
- the organisation of government
- the structure of parliament
- Standing Orders
- the ministerial code and the civil service code and the role of the civil service
- the relationship of Holyrood to local government and other sub-state bodies
- the relationship of Holyrood to Westminster

It is not a sexy, high-constitutional document: *Scotland should be independent* vs *Scotland should remain in the Union* and indeed is indifferent to that question by design.

But it is still a constitutional proposal - on the low constitution side.

It should be taken forward via co-implementation between the Scottish Government and the Scottish Parliament.

Due to the foresight of the drafters of the Scotland Act 1998 this is possible without creating new constitutional institutions by simply using the existing Standing Orders of the Parliament.

Implementation principles

The process that will be used to create the new institutions should be iterative. It should involve systematic testing of the proposals, by:

- building shadow organisations inside the parliament and government
- choosing an uncontentious but appropriate sample bill from the programme for government to pilot
- using existing Standing Orders powers to create an experimental legislative path confined to that chosen single bill.
- executing the process of experimentation
- rinse-repeat until there is consensus on a final state between the Minister for Parliament and the committee members

Having agreed a final state the shadow bodies can:

- instruct parliamentary counsel to prepare the final statutory form for the various components which the Committee can propose to parliament
- define the final state Standing Orders for the Corporate Body to adopt – this includes the standing committee that will need to supervise the Digital Services Scrutiny & Audit Commission and be on point for digital bills
- propose modifications to the 'proper form' for Bill Packs being introduced to parliament to the Corporate Body

In the spirit of *Explicite, Constitutionnalité* and *Simplicité* the development of the new ways of working should be as conservative and non-disruptive as possible, using existing mechanisms and not introducing new ones.

The shadow work can be organised by using existing powers. Working Paper 0.3 *The locus of change* discusses exactly which powers can be used by which body and lays out a roadmap for this implementation plan.

Implementation phases

There should be 5 implementation phases:

- set up of the shadow DSRO
- shadow DSRO and shadow DSS&AC working iteratively
- putting things on a statutory basis
- pause, regroup, grow the extent of the standards world
- mature implementation of new legislative processes for major digital systems

The existence of parliament complicates the programme. Things are either on a statutory basis or they are not.

This implementation plan sidesteps that problem by cutting the Gordian knot.

In the first phase the work should be closely overseen by a Minister with a brief to oversee the shadow organisations and enforce otherwise voluntary nostrums. In the civil service *the Minister wants* is after all a weak form of *the law requires*.

When the work is mature enough the institutions, registers and standards will be transposed from minister-enforced to statutory and the Minister can step back.

There is a considerable amount of, admittedly anecdotal, evidence that younger ministers in countries as varied as Estonia, Ukraine and other parts of Europe have a totally different attitude to digital. In particular they are less englamoured and intimidated by it, less impressed when it is present, and more critical when it is absent.

Phase 1 - Set up of the shadow DSRO

The shadow DSRO is the engine of these institutional changes - and it is involved in almost all of the recommendations.

It should find its feet by implementing the simplest of the uncoupled changes in the following recommendations:

- 1 - *an obligation to publish non-functional & infrastructural statistics about state operations*
- 2 - *Registers of Services, Powers and Policies*
- 6.2 - *changes to the PLU's Bill Handbook*
- 6.3 - *improved organisational support for the PLU and Bill Teams*
- 6.4 - *make non-functional & infrastructural work visible in the Programme for Government*
- 6.7 - *run the strategic research programme and commission new research*
- 6.9 - *a user-centred design roadshow*
- 8.3 - *approvals process for day-to-day services implementation*
- 9 - *a new gazette to publish technical standards in*
- 14 - *testing needs to be made a first class professional discipline in Government*

With relation to the research proposals, the speed at which these should be scheduled will be resource driven.

They have 2 outcomes:

- the results of the research itself
- the civil servants seconded into work on them for 6 months returning to their original department as

change champions having been hothoused/co-located in the shadow DSRO (albeit with CivTech supervision and guidance)

Work can begin on drafting/modelling the first versions of the following recommendations:

- 8.1 - *changes to the Bill Pack for primary legislation*
- 8.2 - *changes to the Explanatory Notes for secondary legislation*
- 15 - *changes to lines of responsibility in the civil service*

This research process has not had the engagement with the parliament as a body that I would have liked. Individual parliamentarians have been happy to engage, but corporate engagement has been lacking.

Historically parliaments have had to fend off interference from overbearing governments so it is not entirely surprising or unexpected.

To move onto co-implementation there will need to be a period of wooing of the parliament by the government. This can happen in the background of Phase 1.

Phase 2 - shadow DSRO and shadow DSS&AC working iteratively

The wooing of parliament having been successful, the meat of the programme can begin.

The parliamentary committee that will be doing the work can be set up in some form. Options for this are discussed in Working Paper 0.3 *The locus of change*.

The experts for the shadow DSS&AC can be recruited and the process of creating the new institution can begin:

- 10 - *create a Digital Services Scrutiny & Audit Commission*

The changes to bill packs and explanatory notes can be tested out. The shadow DSS&AC and the parliamentarians can explore the new legal information architecture.

Temporary Standing Orders can be used to take a sample small Bill and some secondary legislation through the new paths to kick the tyres and test out that things work.

- 8.1 - *changes to the Bill Pack for primary legislation*
- 8.2 - *changes to the Explanatory Notes for secondary legislation*

The committee can be sketching out the legislation to move to a statutory basis, the enactments:

1 - *putting the DSRO on a statutory basis*

2 - *putting the DSS&AC on a statutory basis*

3 - *an Enabling Act*

4 - *new register of services*

5 - *new register of powers*

6 - *new register of policy*

7 - *amendments to The Interpretation And Legislative Reform (Scotland) Act 2011*

In the background the various recommendations that affect the parliament can be put into effect between the Scottish Parliament Corporate Body and the Government:

3 - *widening access to data*

4 - *widening access under research fellowships*

5 - *Short money considerations*

12 - *publication of legislative amendments*

13 - *additional capabilities for SPICe*

DSRO research activities continue on in the background. The DSRO will start acting like a parliament of standards and consulting on standards beyond the basic charter.

PHASE 3 - PUTTING THINGS ON A STATUTORY BASIS

The parliamentary committee that has been doing the work now introduces the various bits of legislation:

1 - *putting the DSRO on a statutory basis*

2 - *putting the DSS&AC on a statutory basis*

3 - *an Enabling Act*

4 - *new register of services*

5 - *new register of powers*

6 - *new register of policy*

7 - *amendments to The Interpretation And Legislative Reform (Scotland) Act 2011*

In addition the necessary changes to the ministerial code, the civil service code and the Osmotherly rules can be promulgated:

15 - *changes to lines of responsibility in the civil service*

DSRO research activities continue on in the background.

PHASE 4 - PAUSE, REGROUP, GROW THE EXTENT OF THE STANDARDS WORLD

The new statutory registers will be operating with very generous *de minimis* at this stage and only covering a fraction of the Scottish state's digital estate.

There will be a period of 12 months where the *de minimis* is wedged down, more systems get caught in the standards net, the DSRO will start work on standards beyond the very primitive ones of the early period.

This period will throw up problems of scale, problems of maturity, problems of glitchy process which all need to be steadily worked through.

The DSRO will need to reorganise itself from the kick-off-and-get-working operating model into its end state target operating model (ToM).

PHASE 5 - MATURE IMPLEMENTATION OF NEW LEGISLATIVE PROCESSES FOR MAJOR DIGITAL SYSTEMS

Once the registers have matured, and there is a high degree of confidence in the institutional structure, work can move onto the remaining big programmes - the recommendations:

- 6.5 - *a law reform process for data*
- 6.6 - *the development and proposition of machinery of government changes*
- The twins:
  - 6.8 - *participation in a joint review of legislative processes with the parliament*
  - 11 - *a review of legislative processes for major digital programmes*
- 7 - *review the process of creating legislation for local government and other sub-state bodies*

and the political capstone in legislation:

- 10 - *a Data Bill of Rights*

How this could fail

The recommendations in this report will fail if they are over-hyped, over-resourced and over-hurried.

In a 100 year framework, five years is a mere bagatelle, work must be slow, prudential, consensual (as befits the constitutional context).

It must be always working, always delivering benefit and start from a small working system.

The team must be the change they want to see: iterative,

humble, transparent, data driven, willing to learn, correct and change course.

Part Four

Notes

A note on Working Papers

A range of working papers were written during this research project. They largely encapsulate necessary technical details which are essential to the proper implementation of these recommendations but which would impede the narrative flow. Some are side-quests.

They are extensively referenced within the text.

WP X	*The heart of the beast*
WP 0.3	*The locus of change*
WP 1.2	*Data and the rule of law*
WP 2	*Rules as code*
WP 3	*The Lego state*
WP 4	*The remixable state*
WP 5.1	*Law reform for data*
WP 6	*A solera for data cleansing*
WP 7.3	*Experimental digital legislative processes*
WP 8	*An Enabling Act*
WP 9.1	*Reading legislation with a non-functional eye*
WP 10.2	*Immediate hygienic measures*
WP 11.1	*Jeff Bezos' API mandate, but for Government*
WP 12	*A Theory of State*
WP 13	*The weak centre*

List of abbreviations

API	Application Programmable Interface
BSI	British Standards Institution
DSS&AC	the new proposed Digital Services Scrutiny & Audit Commission
DSRO	the new proposed Digital Services Reform Office
DWP	Department of Work and Pensions, UK Government
GDaO	Government Data Officer
GDeO	Government Design Officer
GDS	Government Digital Service - the primary UK digital institution
GDPR	General Data Protection Regulation - nominally an EU directive but customarily used for the UK's now-native legislation
GTO	Government Technical Officer
GUI	Graphic User Interface
HMRC	Her/His Majesty's Revenue and Customs - the UK tax authority
ICANN	Internet Corporation For Assigned Names And Numbers
IETF	Internet Engineering Task Force
LGA	Local Government Association - an English and Welsh association of local governments
MoG	Machinery of Government changes
MVP	Minimum Viable Product - often thought of a fully fledged software product, but it can be a paper prototype or something more primitive - here a hypothesis, some success/failure criteria and a means of testing the hypothesis against them

NPS	Net Promoter Score
On-Prem	Short for on-premises - the opposite of in the cloud
PLU	Parliament and Legislation Unit at the Scottish Government
RDS	Research Data Scotland
SAO	Senior Accounting Officers
SG	Scottish Government
SIA	the new proposed Systems Impact Assessment
SO	Standing Order of the Scottish Parliament
SPICe	Scottish Parliament Information Centre
SRO	Senior Responsible Officer
ToM	Target Operating Model

A note on terms

This is a report for Scottish Government - and by default uses Scottish terms (for instance *Programme for Government*, or the use of *Sections* in both Bills and Acts).

Where terms of art that apply to another jurisdiction are used, the relevant jurisdiction will be explicitly mentioned. In the absence of such a qualification, please assume Scotland.

A note on naming and scope

The original brief focused heavily on digital systems, code, databases, GUIs.

A member of a joint Policy/Service Design team and an MSP both challenged me on this.

The first challenge was that I should focus on what the citizen experiences - the service, and not the technology. That challenge was correct and I refocused.

The MSP challenge was that the citizen cares about outcomes not services. That is appropriate for a party-political review, but not a systems and semi-constitutional one.

This report focuses on just a fraction of the work of parliament, and a broadening of approach would open the floodgates to a much larger problem. I have therefore declined to consider outcomes, but remain restricted to capabilities, particularly those enabled by digital systems and services.

A note on AI

There is no explicit mention of AI in this report. AI is already important and transformative in narrow fields.

But we are presented with a vision of general intelligence soon, an AI capable of an explosion of tasks, of creating art, understanding nuance and emotion, thinking independently, reasoning. This is not true, but is it seductive[57].

---

57 In a previous life I ran an ML/AI tools team at a top internet presence. I did customer research on my internal customers and came back with a

Close examination of the big picture of AI reveals it is not continuous, but discrete. There are pixels of use, within a defined domain against a defined problem, with defined high quality data, where Artificial Intelligence, generative or otherwise, and Machine Learning techniques are astonishingly useful. There are more to be discovered.

Like a TV, this gives the impression of real life if viewed at a distance.

It can't pinpoint where those defined domains, problems and data lie in the state - nor would my speculation be fruitful.

This is not an anti-AI position. The 1,000 pages of interview transcripts accumulated in this review had their first pass of transcription done with AI. Every page required extensive manual correction, but doing it all manually would have been even more burdensome.

There will be many point solutions for the application of AI in government.

Institutional structures to provide clean data for use in AI systems is within the scope of this work. Turning that into solutions must be left to the specialists and experts of the civil service.

A note on areas unexplored

This report suffers from a characteristic defect of the

---

small pile and a big pile. The small pile said if we could shift metric X up by Y% then we would see a Z uplift in our revenue line. We think ML/AI applied to this, that and the other data could help us do it. The large pile said I don't like my job and want your brainbox space robots to do it for me. There are a number of areas on political life where AI is being proposed to magically wish away hard problems current age - it is too englamoured by the charisma of technology.

The state must go where the citizen is, and many citizens are on screens. But citizens needs don't start and end there, and lots of people can't use them.

Some elements of this are touched on in the section on research - finding out strategically how the state can orchestrate its services using digital technology for and on behalf of people who can't use it.

The recommendations of this report focus on the tasks done by the three great estaites of the digital age: the technologists, the data specialists and the designers.

And of these three it is the last, the designers, whose work starts with screens and bursts out into the world. Street lamps and road signs, and windows latches and manhole covers were once considered with an artists eye and we shall live in that world again. User journeys and user needs, and lets us say it, citizen pleasures extend into the real and concrete world.

Had we but world enough and time, I would not stop here, but it is at the screen that I must bid my design colleagues *adieu*, and *bonne chance*.

And when I talk narrowly of pre-policy design for infrastructure in this report, I don't believe that precept should be narrowly drawn, we should design the context in which technology is used too.

A note on costs

This report doesn't recommend any capital spend with minor exceptions.[58]

The recommendations fall into one of the following five categories:

- do what we currently do, but in a different sequence
- do what we currently do, but in a different part of the organisation
- do what we currently do, but under different rules
- do what we currently do, but more consistently
- do what we currently do, but with greater velocity

Approximately 15% of all engineering effort on live systems is not feature work, it is maintenance.

In addition new programmes of work that arise in the course of government would be required to be standards compliant.

New programmes of work and the 15% maintenance cost are the continuing financial basis for incrementally moving to standards compliance.

---

58 The 3 exceptions are firstly the R&D programme (6 programmes of 3-5 FTEs of duration 6 months over 3 years). Secondly paying wages for Research Fellowships. Finally the running costs of the Digital Services Scrutiny & Audit Committee. These costs will be of the same order as the Scottish Commission on Social Security - which is budgeting £450,000 for 2024-2025

The DSRO might propose programmes that require up-front capital expenditure to the government, just as the government might instruct the DSRO to do a capital programme. Those capital expenditures would be considered under normal budgetary frameworks.

There are occasions when funding will be needed particularly where recovery of costs by way of fees turns out to be a barrier to uptake. An obvious example[59] of this is Register of Scotland.

The twin body the Digital Service Reform Office is substantially existing functions in the Digital Directorate put on a statutory footing and should be approximately cost-neutral.

59 Section 110 of the Land Registration etc. (Scotland) Act 2012

Interviewees

The following people participated in the research process, as either the subject of a formal interview, being a correspondent, participating in a workshop, or otherwise contributing to the discussion.

I thank them all. This report would not be possible without them, and much of the recommendations comes from them and their work and expertise.

Needless to say, responsibility for the content of the final report lies with me and me alone.

George Adam MSP	Minister for Parliament
Clare Adamson MSP	
Jeffrey Allen	
Derek Alton	Community Insights Lead, Apolitical
Pia Andrews	Executive Director, Digital Government Policy and Innovation for the Department of Finance, Services and Innovation, New South Wales
Esha Sohaib	Policy Officer, Scottish Government

Hedia Balkhi	Senior Design and Research Advisor, Partnerships/Partenariats, Canadian Digital Service/Service numérique canadien
Aileen Baxter	Lead User Researcher, Social Security Scotland
Frances Bell	Parliamentary Counsel, Scottish Government
Nicola Betz	Head of Strategy, Policy and Engagement, Digital Identity One, UK Government
Kenny Birnie	Client Experience Officer, Disclosure Scotland
Joy Bramfitt-Wanless	Deputy Director, Digital Transformation, Scottish Government
Jonathan Brown	Parliamentary Counsel, Scottish Government
Prateek Buch	Head of Collective Intelligence, Policy Lab, UK Government
Lee Bunce	Statistics Policy, Scottish Government
Jeanette Campbell	Special Adviser, Scottish Government
Morag Campsie	Head of Digital Audit, Audit Scotland
Peter Chamberlin	

Robert Colvile	Director, Centre for Policy Studies
Simon Coote	Head of Cross Cutting Policy, Scottish Government
Richard Corbridge	Department for Work and Pensions Digital Group, UK Government
Neil Couling	Director General and Senior Responsible Owner for Universal Credit 2014 to date
Graeme Cowie	Head of the Parliament, Public Administration and Constitution Hub, House of Commons
Ian Davidson	Head of Social Security Policy, Scottish Government
Gemma Diamond	Director of Innovation and Transformation at Audit Scotland
Rachael Dickson	Senior User Researcher, Social Security Scotland
Dr Laurence Diver	Academic Specialist in AI policy, technology regulation and responsible innovation
Laura Duarte	Lead Service Designer, Social Security Scotland

Mark Elliot	CivTech Programme Director, Scottish Government
Becca Fairless	Head of Digital Strategy and Policy, Scottish Government
Matthew Feeney	Head of Tech & Innovation at Centre for Policy Studies
John Fellows	Senior Manager, Digital and Communications, Office of the Scottish Charity Regulator
Dr Jerry Fishenden	Member of the Scottish Government's Online Identity Assurance Expert Group
Tom Forth	CTO at The Data City
Ruth Fox	Director & Head of Research, the Hansard Society
Gavin Freeguard	formerly of the Institute for Government
Charles Garland	Chief Executive of the Scottish Law Commission
Stephen Gethins MP	
Fraser Gough	Parliamentary Counsel, Scottish Government
Alistair Hann	CTO, Scottish Government
Gerard Hart	Disclosure Scotland

Hillary Hartley	former Deputy Minister for Digital, Ottawa
Bridget Hornibrook	DWP Legal Services
Geoff Huggins	Chief Digital Officer, Scottish Government
Dr Abby Innes	Associate Professor in Political Economy, European Institute, LSE
Luke Jeavons	Head of Service Design, Scottish Government
Adrian Kelly	LogLaw
Tom Lamplugh	Head of Social Policy Unit, Scottish Government
Flora Leather	Apprentice Policy Officer, Government of Jersey
Salvador Llopis-quinn	Chief Digital Architect, Scottish Government
Leah Lockhart	Independent Consultant
Richard Lochhead MSP	Minister for Business, Scottish Government
Tom Loosemore	Public Digital, formerly UK Government Digital Service
Steven MacGregor	Head of Parliament and Legislation Unit, Scottish Government
Marida Maiorino	
Michael Marra MSP	

Ivan McKee MSP	Minister for Public Finance, Scottish Government
Eilidh McLaughlin	Deputy Directory, Digital Ethics, Inclusion and Assurance
Ben Macpherson MSP	former Minister for Social Security
John McTernan	
Ann McVie	formerly on the Bill Team, Social Security (Scotland) Act 2019
Denis Merigoux	researcher at INRIA, Paris
Barbara Mills	Deputy Director, Operations and Delivery Management, Scottish Government
Hugh Muschamp	Lead Officer (Climate and Energy), Fife Country Council
Shona Nicol	Team Lead, Data Standards, Scottish Government
Trudy Nicolson	Digital Programme Directory, Scottish Government
Stephen Noon	(former) SPAD, Scottish Government
Louise O'Donnell	Business Architect, Social Security Scotland

Trevor Owen	Head of Human Rights Strategy and Legislation, Scottish Government
Francesca Pagnacco	
Alison Payne	Research Director, Reform Scotland
James Peart	Product Lead - Top75 services in Central Digital & Data Office, UK Government
Eleanor Platt	Senior Data Analyst
Richard Pope	Formerly Government Digital Service
Jayne Purcell	Service Design Lead, Social Security Scotland
Simon Roberts	Improvement Service, Scotland
Esther Roberton	former member of the Consultative Steering Group on the Scottish Parliament
Stuart Roebuck	Principle System Architect, Scottish Government
Steve Roser	
Edward Saperia	Dean of Newspeak House
Lucy Scharbert	Head of legislation and delegated powers at the Scottish Parliament
John Sheridan	Digital Director, UK National Archive

Alex Thomas	Programme Director, Institute for Government
Joe Tree	Head of Product and Accelerator, CivTech, Scottish Government
Willy Van Puymbroeck	Head of Unit, Components, European Commission
Matthew Waddington	Lead for Computer-Readable Legislation Project, Legislative Drafting Office, States of Jersey
Hugh Wallace	Chief Information Officer, Research Data Scotland
Martin Whitfield MSP	
Andy Wightman	Former MSP
Tom Wilkinson	Chief Data Officer, Scottish Government
Gareth Williams	Head of Policy, Prosper
Poppy Wilson	Senior Policy Officer, Scottish Government

PART FIVE

APPENDICES

Appendix 1 - Digital Fellowship Research Proposal

Proposal

A years research programme under the Digital Fellowship Programme.[60]

The research focus will be speed of iteration and continuous improvement and their information flows. It will be end-to-end: from the public sphere, through manifestos, legislation, implementation and daily operations.

The funding outlook looks grim. Comparator countries use digital technology better. Scotland needs to catch-up, improve her capabilities and get better at turning political decisions into world-class operational digital services.

This research proposal is a strategic investment in our capabilities, needed both now and in the future.

The appendix contains a number of hypotheses, the evidence that supports and informs them and sketches of the programme to explore them. Obviously the research will follow the evidence uncovered.

Interviewees and participants

The interviewees and participants in the research will half in Scotland/half furth of Scotland:

- Election teams of all parties
- Think tankers and other appropriate public intellectuals
- Ministers (past and present)
- Non-ministerial Parliamentarians (all parties)
- Relevant members of statutory and parliamentary

60 https://www.gov.scot/policies/digital/digital-fellowship/

corporate bodies

• Civil servants (Scotland, UK ,Canada, the US, Australia and the Nordics)

• Academics/practitioners (including those working in the "code as law" field)

Requirements

• a ministerial sponsor

• a civil service sponsor

Outputs

• a set of recommendations for the Scottish Government

• a book aimed at the lay informed political reader - with worked examples from Scotland

• a weekly free-to-air newsletter on Substack - necessary to recruit and engage globally.

The Ask

The ask of the Scottish government is:

• access - to officials and minsters for interviews, to internal documents

• a desk, pass, network connection

• the 'charisma' of the Digital Fellowship to help secure participation from outsiders

Digital Fellowships are unpaid - I am retired and have no conflicts of interest.

Curriculum Vitae

Politics

Policy development in Scotland, England and NI, Holyrood and Westminster candidate, electoral computing expert, pre-manifesto work on the Glasgow local council campaign.

Industry

IT Strategy at RBS/DLFS, Chief Technical Architect at if.com, Scottish startup sector, stability guru at the UK's biggest internet firm bet365.com, VP Eng at Silicon Valley-backed firm in Berlin.

Public Service

Public sector experience with Edinburgh City Council/BT and Scottish Enterprise.

OneTeamGov - the global public service network and other grassroots and practitioners bodies.

Books

Scotland After Brexit[61] and War Is Coming[62]

---

61 https://www.amazon.co.uk/Winning-Second-Independence-Referendum-Manifesto-ebook/dp/B01LXWK08G

62 https://www.amazon.co.uk/War-Coming-Gordon-Guthrie-ebook/dp/B01ETH91PY

Appendix 2 - Digital Fellowship research axioms and hypotheses

Axiom 1

The Scottish political class are not good enough customers of digital services (yet). Prior to 1983 almost no legislation anywhere in the world led to the creation of a computer system, now almost no legislation doesn't. Systems do not optimally do things they were not designed to.

Evidence

Nigel Smith chaired[63] the steering group that designed the Scottish Parliament's procedures and I asked him.

Axiom 2

We already have the answers, we don't necessarily know it.

Northcote-Trevelyan[64] didn't create any new practices - implicit practices became explicit and departmental practices became universal.

Hypothesis 1

Continuous improvement via process re-ordering will identify defects earlier, reduce iteration time and lead to better outcomes.

Proposition

The current flow look like this:

---

63 Further discussion with Esther Robertson led us to the conclusion that Nigel Smith had misremembered in the short pamphlet he wrote shortly before his death - he sat on a working group looking at use of IT in making the internal processes of Holyrood accessible remotely.

64 https://www.civilservant.org.uk/library/1854_Northcote_Trevelyan_Report.pdf

```
Manifesto -> White Paper -> Bill -> Act ->
Paper Prototype -> Alpha -> Beta -> In Service
```

Service design with prototyping and iteration is post-legislative. Late caught defects are more expensive to fix and lead to slower delivery. Can we bring those iterative activities (paper prototyping, alpha and beta) earlier? Perhaps a process with staged parliamentary approvals:

```
Manifesto -> White Paper -> Paper Prototype ->
Stage 1 -> Alpha -> Stage 2 -> Beta -> Act -> In
Service
```

Evidence

I have socialised this thesis in the Service Design community and with Cabinet Office civil servants: the response has been positive.

See also Edinburgh Trams - Phase 1 Vs Phase 2.

Research Methodologies

Create a paper-prototype by screenshotting an operational system and copying its operational manuals and use these to gameplay proposed transformed legislative processes.

HYPOTHESIS 2

The legislative process contains hidden barriers to modernisation.

Evidence

In 2003 the troubleshooter Peter Gershon[65] reviewed Labour's public sector transformation programme which had promised big cost saving. He cut all digital transformation that needed primary legislation.

The final programme saved L20bn - L18.5bn of back-office

---

65 https://www.civilservant.org.uk/library/2004_gershon_releasing_resources_to_the_front_line.pdf

efficiencies, L500m electronic payments and only L1bn citizen-facing. Efficient Government in Scotland yielded only L85m citizen-facing out of L1.7bn.

In the tech sector customer-facing savings have dwarfed back-office by a considerable margin.

Research Methodologies

Interview Gershon and participants. Interview ministers about their ambitions ("be more like Estonia").

HYPOTHESIS 3

Legislation implicitly defines data and hence processes in the administrative state.

Proposition

Greater clarity at the system design stage will come from making data handling an explicit first class component of legislative drafting and this will lead to cost savings and service improvement.

Evidence

The Bichard[66] report into the Soham Murders focussed on Ian Huntley's vetting check - a microscopic view of the 17 databases and the regulation and legislation they implemented and how the different social services and police departments interacted.

It is forensic in its discussion of operational failures: in data deletion ('weeding'), in indexing, and in unrecorded information.

The specification of computer systems by legislation and regulation is clearly visible in the report.

Research Methodology

---

66 https://dera.ioe.ac.uk/id/eprint/6394/1/report.pdf

Bichard took a deep vertical look - a shallow and wide view needs to be taken. Identify a current system and the legislation and regulations that define it and rewrite them in a proposed new explicit format and workshop them - create a paper prototype of a new legislative language.

Hypothesis 4

The audit structure for administrative legislation needs to be extended.

Proposition

The defining nature of now is digital goods and services. That is driven by user choice in the private sector: best, cheapest, easiest, most convenient. But the public sector uses compulsion: you must pay tax, register your car.

This creates new time-taxes for citizens, and the forces for improvement are politics not purchasing. Without appropriate information of user behaviour patterns those pathways are blocked. Waiting times for hospitals is a staple topic in the public sphere, waiting times on government websites or call centres isn't.

Evidence

The modern state birthed the modern bill pack. Services are created by legislation - and financial impact statements are required. They are funded ongoing by a separate legislative stream. There is statutory audit.

By comparison, continuous improvement lacks a similar long-running audit function. Government departments currently mark their own user-experience homework.

Research Methodology

Paper prototypes of new audit oversight can be mocked up from existing internal operational and management information decks and these can be game played with parliamentarians, journalists and external public actors.

Appendix 3 - Research precepts

The research was informed by 10 precepts:

1. *Against detachment*. This is not anthropology. The author is also a practitioner - a practitioner in public policy, a politician manqué[67], and a career technologist. Practitioner interviews can provide material, understanding and problem definitions. The systems thinking and synthesis must be done by a practitioner.
2. *People rarely fail, processes often fail*. The assumption was that civil servants are dedicated public servants and work in good faith inside the system and processes that exist. No blamestorming.
3. *Experience over seniority*. Proximity to the work on the ground is critical.
4. *Pro synthesis, contra innovation*. With millions of civil servants wrestling with the same problems, solutions were to be found in existing work, in Scotland, in the UK, across the world.
5. *A prejudice for precedents*. There is nothing new under the sun. The problems we have are new versions of older ones. The solutions should rhyme with previous solutions.
6. *An unnatural love for the Goldilocks question*. Should this decision be taken at this point in the cycle, or earlier or later? And if now is the right time, should it be taken by this person, their senior or their junior?
7. *Pro core competencies*. Organisations should do their core competencies. Design (organisational, service,

---

[67] manqué sounds so much better than failed

user experience, content and more) and software development are core competencies alongside policy development. Outsourcing them to private firms is a false economy. The commercial partner learns by building and delivering and not the state.

8. *Contra reading over from the private sector.* Government isn't the private sector. Government can't act the same way as the private sector. Civil servants inhabit a different environment from their private sector counterparts. Lessons can be learnt, processes can rhyme, but things will be different. *Government is government.*
9. *Contra centralisation and central planning*. The besetting sin of the British state at all levels including Scotland is centralisation. In addition New Public Management tried to bring market mechanisms into the state. It also recognised that they were ill-suited, and tried to address that by building a regulatory framework that could mimic a real market. As Abby Innes has pointed out so eloquently[68] the resulting centralised apparatus resembles the old Soviet Gosplan.

---

68 Innes, A. (2023) *Late Soviet Britain: Why Materialist Utopias Fail*, Cambridge University Press, 2023

10. *Build a simple working system first.* Gall's Law states:

> *A complex system that works is invariably found to have evolved from a simple system that worked. A complex system designed from scratch never works and cannot be patched up to make it work. You have to start over with a working simple system.*

Appendix 4 - A short history of the bill pack and financial resolution

The modern control mechanisms for development of legislative systems are comparatively sophisticated. Each functional bill is accompanied through parliament by a parallel financial resolution which effectively has a veto role on commencement. If we regard data as a state asset, and code as a state liability then some sort of parallel management process that rhymes with the financial one suggests itself.

The bill pack is the place where non-functional & infrastructural specifications can be added to functional ones. With the charisma[69] of ministers behind it, the civil service will fall in line.

To that end the history and origin of the modern bill pack was investigated.

Until 1875 and the birth of structured legislation, bills were simply slabs of code and structure was applied to them in the reading.

The 1875 Militia Bill marks the birth of the modern bill pack. It tidied up a raft of older legislation. Each clause of the bill was preceded by a heading and the whole bill had a table of contents at the beginning - termed a breviate. These decorations on the face of the bill were struck out on its passage through to Royal Assent.

Gradually that breviate and those headings became the standard form of structured legislation and the core of the

---

69 Don't embarrass your Minister being the 11th commandment of the Civil Service

modern bill pack. The financial memorandum and modern financial controls come relatively late in 1927.

Changes to parliamentary procedure recommended in this report will be similarly slow and iterative. In a 100 year project, three to five years is plenty fast.

There is a discussion of the history of the Bill Pack with select examples in the appendix of Working Paper 10.2 *Immediate Hygienic Measures*.

Appendix 5 - Failure to manage non-functionals/infrastructurals in the public sector

A WORKED EXAMPLE FROM THE PUBLIC SECTOR - LAND INFORMATION SERVICES

Further evidence of the inability of the state to manage non-functionals/infrastructurals comes from a retrospective of a long running failure dating back to the 1990s.

In a long report called *ScotLIS 3 - a critical tool for Scotland: Scotland's land information service: what it is and why it matters*[70] for the David Hume Institute, the former MSP Andy Wightman laid out the sorry tale of joined-up land information.

The ending is given away by the title - ScotLIS 3 is the proposed implementation that ScotLIS and ScotLIS 2 never delivered.

The first attempt was in the 1990s. Its failure is perhaps understandable[71]. A pilot was produced but not proceeded with.

A delivery plan[72] for ScotLIS 2 was requested in 2017 by the then DFM John Swinney:

---

70 https://static1.squarespace.com/static/59b82ed532601e01a494df34/t/64075b6d50ab33464b4bfbf6/1678203757948/SCOTLIS+Report+by+Andy+Wightman+March+2023.pdf

71 Mapping technology was both much more expensive In 1998 I built a geomapping prototype for electioneering as part of Scottish Computing For Labour - the base costs were £1,500 per user, per constituency - plus a new computer to run the software on. And much more primitive 30 years ago.

72 https://www.ros.gov.uk/about/publications/governance-and-corporate/2015/digital-land-and-property-information-system-report-july-2015

> *In March 2015, the Deputy First Minister announced his commitment to Scotland having an easy-to-use and affordable system for accessing a wide range of information about land and property - a "one-stop-digital database for land and information services". He asked that work on this be taken forward in a collaborative manner through a taskforce headed by the Keeper of the Registers of Scotland and involving, amongst others, the Improvement Service, Scottish Government, Ordnance Survey, and Unifi Scotland, and that the taskforce should provide him with a report on how this can best be delivered by 31 July 2015.*

The plan was to launch by 2017 - and it indeed launched then. However the only data on it was from the Land Register (a statutory function with a legal functional requirement - a *Must Have*). None of the integration that would allow other geographical data sets to seamlessly work with it happened (the non-functional & infrastructural requirements - the *Nice To Haves*).

In Andy Wightman's report he concludes:

> *ScotLIS has thus taken an important first step in acting as an effective portal for searching the Land Register. However, progress on completing the remaining elements of the first wave stalled and have not been delivered. This is not the fault of the Registers of Scotland or indeed of any of the other organisations represented on the taskforce. In a roundtable discussion that informed this paper, there was a consensus among participants that there has been a failure of political leadership, in particular to establish the governance*

framework necessary to deliver the ambitions set out in 2015.

Since then new land registers have been created by statute - and delivered unjoined.

Andy Wightman makes the following points about data integration in his report:

1. Some data[73] *is unavailable beyond a restricted group of users. The most prominent example of this is a wide range of datasets including Forestry and Woodland Strategies, Gritting Routes, GP Practices and Cycling Networks that form part of the Spatial Hub administered by the Improvement Service but to which access is restricted to Public Sector Geospatial Agreement (PGSA) members. All of this is information has been collected and aggregated at public expense.*

2. Some data[74] *is available to all but only via a web interface designed by the data holder. The raw data is not available for use by anyone outside the organisation. The Valuation Roll held by the Scottish Assessors is a good example of such a restricted dataset.*

3. Some data[75] *is held but not in an easily accessible format. For example, the Register of Persons Holding a Controlled Interest in Land is not searchable by a map and is not integrated with other land and property information held by the same organisation.*

4. Some data is held but in an inconsistent and unreliable manner. For example, the sale of a crofting

---

73 https://data.spatialhub.scot/dataset/

74 https://www.saa.gov.uk/

75 https://rci.ros.gov.uk/

common grazing in Argyll which is agreed between the landowner and shareholders has been delayed for two years because of inadequate records documenting the identity of every shareholder.

5. Some data is simply not available at all, for example, the location and extent of land held under agricultural tenancies or data on the construction and condition of the built environment.

The process failings which Andy Wightman identifies in ScotLIS are an instance of the general problem of management of non-functional & infrastructural requirements. The goal of this report is to fix all the problems of this type, not just this instance.

He further identifies issues in delivering it:

One challenge is putting in place the appropriate governance framework with appropriate political leadership to make it happen. This appears to have been the key failing in the delivery of the stated ambitions for ScotLIS.

In the absence of an analytical framework to define the right governance it is to be expected that this failing will occur. It is not, and cannot be the job of elected members to be masters and designers of technical governance.

Another challenge is ensuring that the data to be collated can be used for purposes other than that for which it is collected. There may be some legislative changes needed but these are believed to be modest.

That issue is addressed[76] in this report.

---

[76] It is discussed in some detail in Working Paper 8 - *An Enabling Act* which proposes a fast track legislative process to manage retrofitting legal

> *There is also the technical challenge of collating data in a modern format for integration into ScotLIS. That is a challenge that has been successfully met in many other systems of land administration.*

This is an enforcement problem and not a technical challenge. The *right thing* is known but is only a *Nice To Have*.

> *Finally, there is a financial challenge in both paying for the development of ScotLIS and in ongoing administration. No estimates of costs are provided in the 2015 paper but this is probably the least of the challenges. It is in the interests of the public sector to be collecting and maintaining datasets in as efficient a manner as possible. The technical means exist to integrate this into a one-stop portal and charging regimes for data can still be implemented. For the consumer, it is not the fees to obtain data that cause frustration so much as the time and associated expense of doing so.*

There is a fundamental cost of rework. Systems implemented in silos must be re-engineered to work jointly.

As the old joke has it - *there's never money to do it right, there's always money to do it twice*. The point of the standards regime recommended in this report is to *do it right the first time*.

But software is still incurring a maintenance cost - typically 15% of the IT spend - software needs to be patched up, maintained, tweaked and replaced.

---

changes under the formal parliamentary oversight mechanism proposed in Working Paper 0.3 - *The locus of change*.

With a permissive standards regime this maintenance work that is going to be done and paid for anyway can be used to bring existing systems into line without a major expansion in cost, if you are willing to wait.

Appendix 6 - CivTech Research Proposals

Generating MVPs as part of policy and legislative design

This proposal is a rerun of work done in New Zealand in 2018 by their Service Innovation Lab in a project called *Better Rules And Legislation As Code.*[77]

That work was a lawyer-led approach to rethinking the development of law to enable simpler and better development of regulations, entitlements and calculations.

They pioneered cross-organisational working with parliamentary counsel, policy makers, service designers and delivery people working in multi-disciplinary teams.

The project also identified and struck down key barriers between policy intent and deliverability and demonstrated value and velocity by using Rules as Code.

They demonstrated that Rules as Code tech can be used as way of building quick prototyping tools that enable fast design feedback loops in the development of policy and legislation – having a common 'surface' that members of different professions can engage with is an excellent tool for collapsing getting-on-the-same-page discussions and associated costs.

Because we already know that this approach works, the objectives and outcomes of this research project are:

- a profound understanding of using Rules as Code in this way
- a training programme to roll it out across policy

77 https://serviceinnovationlab.github.io/projects/legislation-as-code/

makers and legislative teams in Scotland

- an integrated change-management plan to make it a permanent feature of legislative development

Possible partners in this project are the New Zealand Service Innovation Lab themselves and the team at the DWP around Barbara Hornibrook who are building calculators/explainers for Universal Credit.

See also Working Paper 2 *Rules as code.*

MACRO-ECONOMIC MODELLING

For highly numeric and procedure bound administrative law (social security, tax) there is a fairly detailed representation in legislation of the ***Thing*** (people or organisations and their circumstances) that can be faithfully mapped[78] to the ***Model*** (the data that represents them in a computer system). (see the discussion in Working Paper 5.1 *Law reform for data*).

With properly annotated legislation it is then possible to compile it to a set of calculation libraries that faithfully execute the appropriate calculations.

> *Jean is a single mother of 2 children aged 5 and 7, one of whom has special needs. Her income is £2,494 per month, her entitlement therefore is...*

This research proposal is to look at the integration of those libraries into existing macro-economic models. With a correct statistical overview of society that has the right mix of social circumstances and income realistic models of money flows can be built.

---

78 The issues and problems of relating law to data are covered in extensive detail in Working Paper 5.1 *Law reform for data* - particularly sections 3 and 4

The idea here is that changes to social security and tax could be drafted in legislative form, that draft could be compiled and integrated into a macro model which could then be examined to see its macro-effects, cliffs and cut-offs, winners and losers, etc.

Adjustments to tax and social security could then be subject to fast iteration at the design stage - with the final regulations being released to parliament backed by detailed modelling.

Parliamentary amendments could similarly be tested.

The outcomes of this would be a proof of concept with existing Scottish Government modellers.

Possible partners include the Catala team in INRIA in Paris under Denis Merigoux who have prototyped this in France.

See also Working Paper 2 *Rules as code.*

Property-based testing

This research project is the odd-one out of this entire report. It is purely functional - whereas the rest of the recommendations are non-functional & infrastructural.

It also explicitly lacks a precedent in the public sector and has been read across from the private sector and thus it violates some of the prejudices and precepts on which this research was founded. It does have some major private sector precedents - which I have worked on.[79] The realisation that

---

79 Universal Credit is a major programme distributing £1bn every 9 days. It is mostly asynchronous with some soft-realtime components and runs in 2 jurisdictions (England&Wales and Scotland) and 2 languages. bet365 in 2014 turned over $600m a week ($600m in, $582m out, margins of 3%). It was mostly soft-real time and ran in 80+ jurisdictions and 80+ languages. Finger in the air, UC and bet365 are systems at the same scale. The SQL databases at bet365 were maxed out and had to be ripped out and replaced with a NoSQL datastore. I designed the testing protocol, using the techniques under investigation here, we

legislation is purely functional unlocked the problem. Who was managing the non-functional & infrastructural requirements?

It uses Rules as Code not to generate production code, but production tests. This approach can rip out both time and money from major projects.

There are some hard technical issues to be resolved though before it can be used in the public sector in this way.

The outputs would be a test generator with testing framework and a working multi-programming language framework for mapping the point-of-application of a test to a URL.

See also Working Paper 2 *Rules as code*.

Reducing barriers to legislative compliance

This proposal uses Rules as Code to build reference systems for regulatory compliance.

A superpower of major tech companies is procedure-as-code, creating click-button systems that co-ordinate and deliver complex processes spanning thousands of servers in hundreds of data centres across the world.

This project explores using regulation-as-code to remove the cost of regulation by removing some of the *compliance costs* but retaining the *regulation*.

The process is similar to that outlined in the macro-economic model research programme. Legislation is drafted and compiled into a simple reference system. That system is then shared with industry in the regulated sector at the pre-

---

generated 8 million tests and a team of 12 and built and deployed the solution with no down time in 6 months. bet365 now turns over $2bn a week. Consequently I am confident that the process being explored in this research project has the potential to be enormously useful for major IT deliveries in the public sector.

legislative stage and adjusted based on their feedback.

The goal is to achieve a win-win, regulations that have the appropriate social, environmental or economic impact whilst being low cost to the people being regulated.

Regulation acts as a moat around the markets for regulated products - keeping new smaller competitors out. This has the effect of keeping margins and prices for regulated products high. Reducing the barriers to entry, whilst retaining the benefits of regulation, by releasing example implementations alongside the new regulations should unleash competition and price reduction.

It should be remembered however, that the example implementations generated here are not the law represented-in-code. The final say on legality or otherwise of regulated systems remains the courts.

The outcome would be a regulatory system compiled into a prototype and used to test the validity of this approach with partners from the regulated industry in question.

This is being looked at the Bank of England - a possible partner in this research.

See also Working Paper 2 *Rules as code.*

Components

Working Paper 3 *The Lego state* outlines a model of componentisation. This is a known and deployed technique. Patterns in one domain are converted to products in another and promoted up the value chain.

An example would be the Government Design System components.[80]

80 https://design-system.service.gov.uk/components/

These represent a journey from guidelines saying this is how to design buttons and forms well to saying here is a set of html5, javascript and css files that are precanned components - use them.

Because of the location of GDS in the organisational structure of Whitehall, the component publication journey ends at UX design.

Working Paper 3 *The Lego state* outlines a much more expansive set of components, including legislative patterns and fully configurable software systems - but the development and promotion journey remains similar.

The outcome of this project is a set of procedures, training and working components that can be deployed across the appropriate parts of the Scottish civil service so that componentisation becomes something that Scotland just does.

REMIXABILITY

Working Paper 4 *The remixable state* outlines a proposal for using delegated identity and the separation of line of business systems from workflow systems around service-based architectures to imagine a radically different future for the Scottish state over the next 100 years.

The goal of this research project would be to produce some small prototypes of systems showing the use of delegated authority and sketching out an architecture of remix and refocus.

Having done that, the working MVPs should be taken on a policy roadshow to assess if this style of approach is appropriate.

The use case recommended is for 80/20 services where 80% of the population can happily self-serve on line, but

20% have more complex needs and need supporting through it, particularly in the context of access to multiple services.

Revisiting on-prem and global scale capacity

Government is moving over to the cloud because of the perceived benefits of using the orchestration and deployment stacks of major tech companies. This brings with it tremendous capabilities but also risks and dependencies. The disturbed political situation in the United States means that continuing dependency on US-based providers remains a risk. There are political and regulatory pressures to on-shore data.

Recent developments[81] indicate that the market for orchestration and deployment might be commodifying. Scottish government should investigate this in a research spike.

---

81 The parent company of Lidl has launched a cloud computing service for the German and Austrian market, and new companies like Oxide Computing are developing data centre sleds with in-built orchestration, managed VPNs, deployment management and security, etc, etc with a goal to delivering in-cloud capability on-prem at commodity prices.

Printed in Dunstable, United Kingdom

81935981R00127